The New
Encyclopedia
of
KNOTS

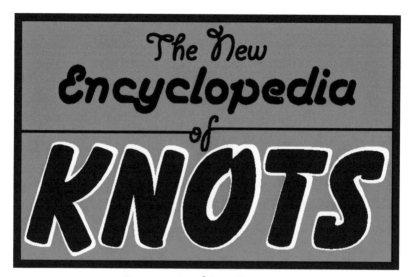

The New Encyclopedia of KNOTS

Derek E. Avery

BROCKHAMPTON PRESS

First published in Great Britain by
Brockhampton Press
a member of
the Hodder Headline Group
20 Bloomsbury Street
London WC1B 3QA

ISBN 1 86019 190 8

Reprint 1998

Designed and produced by
Superlaunch Ltd
PO Box 207
Abingdon
Oxfordshire OX13 6TA, England
Printed in Hong Kong / China

Author's note

There are strict regulations governing the use of wire eye splices in industry, and although certain knots are considered adequate for normal usage, you should always refer to the regulations in force at the time.

Never hold fish hooks in your bare hands; always use pliers to hold them firmly. Similarly, always be careful to wear heavy gloves or to wrap your hands in rags before pulling on thin monofilament lines or twine. This both avoids cutting your flesh and helps to give a better grip on the line.

The descriptions of the methods for tying all of the knots included here assume right-handedness, as individuals vary so much in their degree of ambidexterity.

Where a knot has been illustrated, it has been given a number working numerically from the beginning of the book. When more than one step has been illustrated in making a knot, the illustration number has been suffixed; thus the second step under the entry for binder turn is *figure 11.2*.

A

Admiralty eye splice: a wire splice generally considered adequate for normal industrial usage, the main feature of which is that after the first tuck, all strands are tucked away in an 'over one, under one' sequence, against the lay of the standing part.

There are also various ways of completing the first full tuck, the most common of which is in the strand order of 1–6–2–3–5–4.

First establish the size of the eye and apply a seizing accordingly. Then unlay the strands to the required length, ensuring that they are in the correct order. The illustration (*figure 1*) shows the relative positions of the tucking strands to the standing part.

figure 1

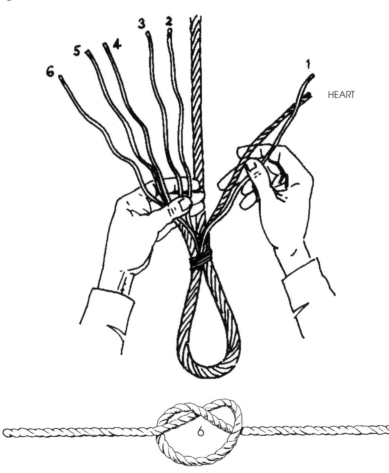

HEART

The heart is always associated with strand 1, which is the first to be tucked and which is worked from left to right, over one and under one, with the standing part to the right. A marline spike or hollow splicing tool is used to separate the strands for tucking. After strand 1 has been tucked and hauled tight the heart can be cut out. Strand 6 is then tucked, also from left to right and also in an over one, under one sequence, and hauled tight. Strand 2 is worked from right to left, going around the same strand of the standing part as strand 6, but as it is progressing in the opposite direction it provides a locking turn when the strand is hauled tight. Strand 3 is worked from right to left, as is the next strand (5), but this strand breaks the established over and under sequence by being tucked under two strands initially. The final strand, 4, follows the previous strand (5) but reverts to the sequence of over one and under one, emerging between the two strands of the standing part that strand 5 had been tucked under. This completes the first tuck, and you can now continue, with all strands tucked over one and under one against the lay. Five full tucks are usual,

and each strand should be hammered down with a mallet after each tuck.

Anchor bend *see* **bucket hitch**.

Anchoring *see* **belaying to a mooring bollard or samson post**.

B

figure 2

Back splice: a splice used to prevent the end of a rope from unlaying. It starts with a crown knot (page 57), after which each strand is tucked three times back down the standing part (*figure 2*).

figure 3

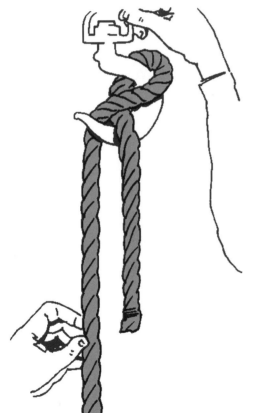

Backwall hitch: a simple, quick and efficient method for attaching the tail of a rope to a hook. It relies upon a constant strain being maintained, but it will slip unless the knot is held in position while the strain is taken up (*figure 3*).

Bare end *see* **bitter end**.

Bargee's eye splice: perhaps this is the simplest of splices, providing a rough and ready yet quite effective eye (*figure 4.1*), with the end of the rope tucked once through a single strand of the standing part (*figure 4.2*).

Barrel knot *see* **blood knot**.

Becket bend *see* **sheet bend**.

Belaying: the method by which ropes are made fast on board ship and from ship to shore, by winding the rope under load in a figure-of-eight pattern around a fixture.

Belaying a rope with a cleat, or **cleating**, requires three or four cross turns of the rope, which passes under the horns of the cleat, crosses above the cleat (*figures 5.1 and 5.2*)and finishes with a half hitch (*figure 5.3*). This prevents the turns from falling off as the result of the boat's motion. It is

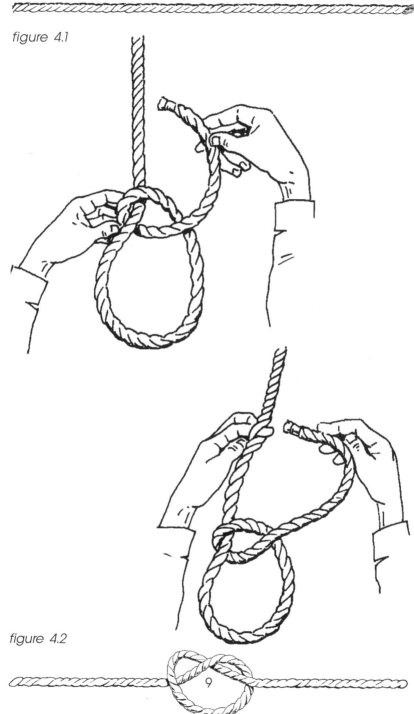

figure 4.1

figure 4.2

9

figure 5.1

figure 5.2

important that no load is applied to the half hitch, as this could result in jamming, making untying difficult. The half hitch is applied to the upper horn of the cleat, if the cleat is vertical.

Belaying a rope to a belaying pin is carried out in much the same way as when cleating. Make a start to the right of the pin with a full round turn taken clockwise around the pin; turns should always be

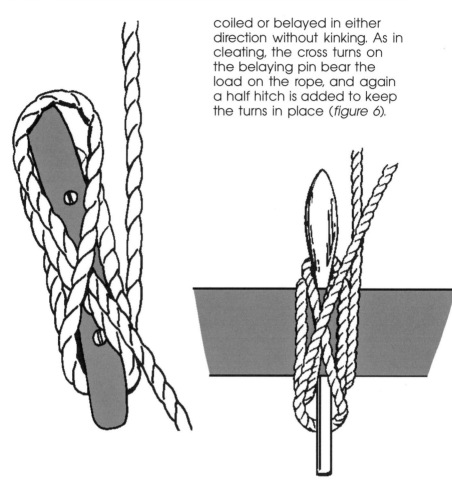

coiled or belayed in either direction without kinking. As in cleating, the cross turns on the belaying pin bear the load on the rope, and again a half hitch is added to keep the turns in place (*figure 6*).

figure 5.3

figure 6

taken in the same direction as that in which the rope is coiled. This prevents the strands from being forced open, and the rope will kink less. This does not apply to braided rope, which can be

Belaying to a mooring bollard or samson post secures a ship to shore. Take a series of turns around the post, and pass a bight of rope under the (load-bearing) standing part and then drop it over the turns on

figure 7

the post (*figure 7*). You can take the end around the post again, and pass another bight under the standing part to drop it over the post. You can repeat the process again, but on no account should you take a turn around the post with the standing part.

A bollard with a pair of horizontal arms is known as a **staghorn**, and you can make fast a mooring line to a staghorn by taking the line around the bollard, up over one arm (*figure 8.1*), down, and back across the same side of the bollard and up over the other arm, returning across the same side of the bollard again in a figure-of-eight pattern (*figure 8.2*), repeating the sequence until the line is secure. This method, which is sometimes called anchoring, permits the line to be cast off even while it is under load.

figure 8.1

figure 8.2

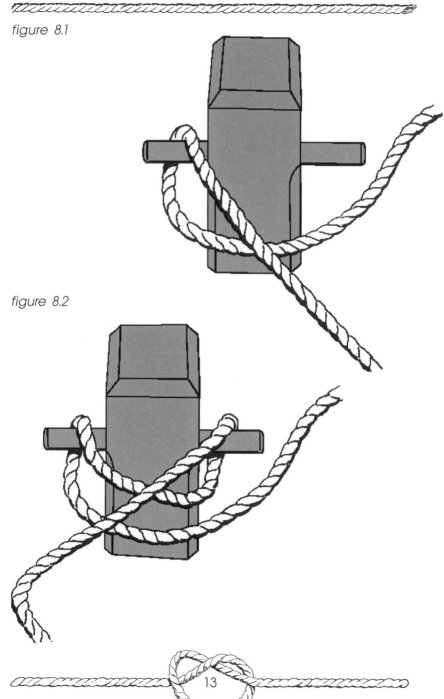

Bend: a knot which ties together the ends of two free ropes, or the action of knotting two ropes together; one rope is said to be 'bent to' another; *see also* buntline fisherman's bend, carrick bend, double carrick bend, double sheet bend, heaving line bend, hunter's bend, sheet bend; for fisherman's bend, *see* bucket hitch.

Bight: the slack part of a rope, formed between either end and the standing part, which is not entirely straight (*figure 9*); any loop or curvature, to the maximum of a full circle. Any point within the curve is said to be 'in the bight'. If a knot is tied 'on the bight', the rope ends are not required for the tying process.

figure 9

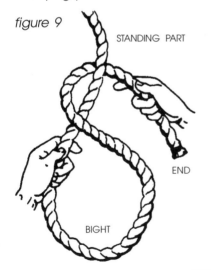

STANDING PART

END

BIGHT

figure 10.1

Bimini twist, twenty times around knot or **double line loop:** an angler's knot, that when tied in nylon monofilament or braided line is claimed to be 100% efficient, or as strong as the unknotted line. It is commonly used by anglers as the basis

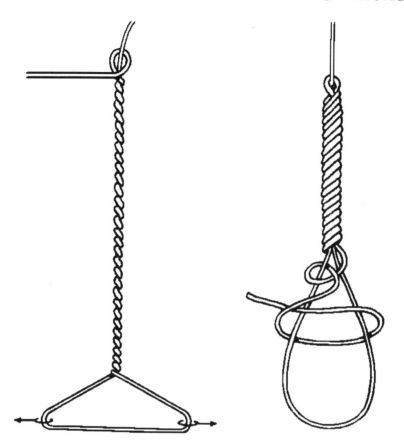

figure 10.2   figure 10.3

for most of their knot systems.

Form a large bight, perhaps as much as a metre (yard) long, and hold the standing part and the end in your right hand, while placing your other hand within the bight to twist the end around the

standing part twenty times. You should then lay the bight on the ground, and stand with your feet on the line (*figure 10.1*). Meanwhile, transfer the standing part only to your now-free left hand; the working end remains in your right hand.

Move your feet slightly apart to enlarge the loop and force the twists in the standing part and the working end to tighten. Meanwhile pull the standing part and the working end firmly, keeping your hands apart and at an angle of 45 degrees above the last twist in the line. Resist the tendency to lower your hands.

This angle forces the twists tightly together, so that the working end which you are holding in your right hand can now be lowered, almost to form a right-angle with the twists (*figure 10.2*). If you slacken the tension just a little on the standing part, this will enable it to jump back over the first twist. Now move your feet slowly farther apart, so that the tension created will force the line to roll down over the twists in parallel coils as you feed the standing part slowly into the twists so that they lie evenly and parallel to each other. When this layer of riding turns is complete, finish off with a half hitch around a single part of the bight and then a second half hitch around both parts (*figure 10.3*).

Binder turn: a less well-known variation of the sheet bend, with similar applications. It is a

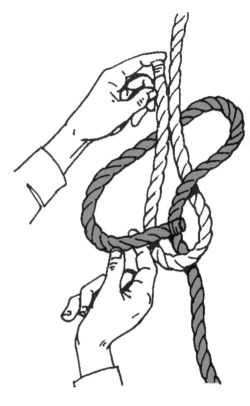

figure 11.1

very useful knot for joining two ropes of different thicknesses, when the larger rope should provide the bight and the smaller rope provides the bends or turns. It has the added advantage that one of the standing parts and the two tails lie together on the same side, which make it a suitable knot for working close to a block.

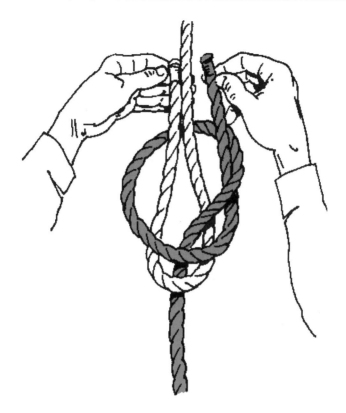

figure 11.2

Make a bight in one end of the rope and weave the second rope up through the bight from the back. Continue around the back of the bight (*figure 11.1*), around the front and up between the standing part of the first rope and its own first loop (*figure 11.2*). When you pull the knot tight, the two tails lie together with the standing part of the first

rope.

Bitter end, bare end or **tag end** : the end of the rope with which you are working (*figure 12*); *see also* tail.

Blood bight: a loop knot favoured by anglers, which is no more than a simple stopper knot tied on the bight and therefore very easy to tie.

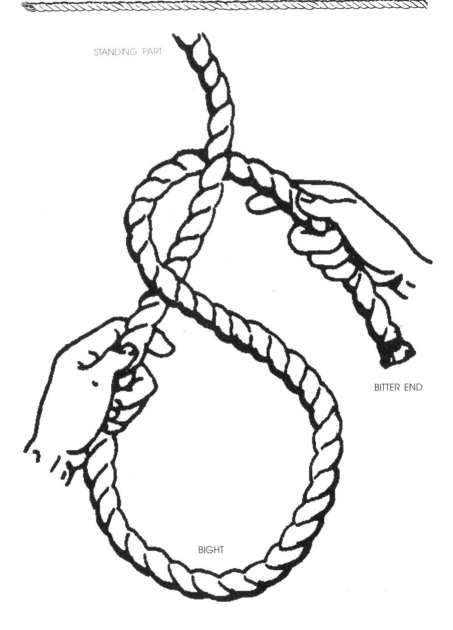

STANDING PART

BITTER END

BIGHT

figure 12

Double the end of the line, holding the standing part and the end in your left hand. Form a loop, by bringing the end of this bight back, around and over itself, and hold this between the thumb and forefinger of your left hand, with the standing parts. Now take two twists in the loop, clockwise, to produce a 360 degree turn. This can be done most easily by placing your right forefinger down into the head of the loop to keep it taut, and winding your finger in an imaginary circle. Complete the knot by bringing the end of the bight from your left hand up through the eye of the loop and hauling it tight.

Blood knot or **barrel knot:** a group of knots used by anglers, all of which have a large number of wrapping turns to provide a relatively high breaking strength. The blood knot is suitable for connecting lines of different sizes, although if the sizes vary greatly the improved blood knot (*see* page 98) should be used.

Take the two lines from opposing sides and cross them to form an X. Squeeze the point where they cross

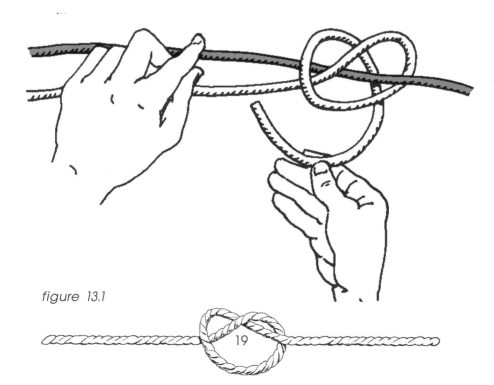

figure 13.1

figure 13.2

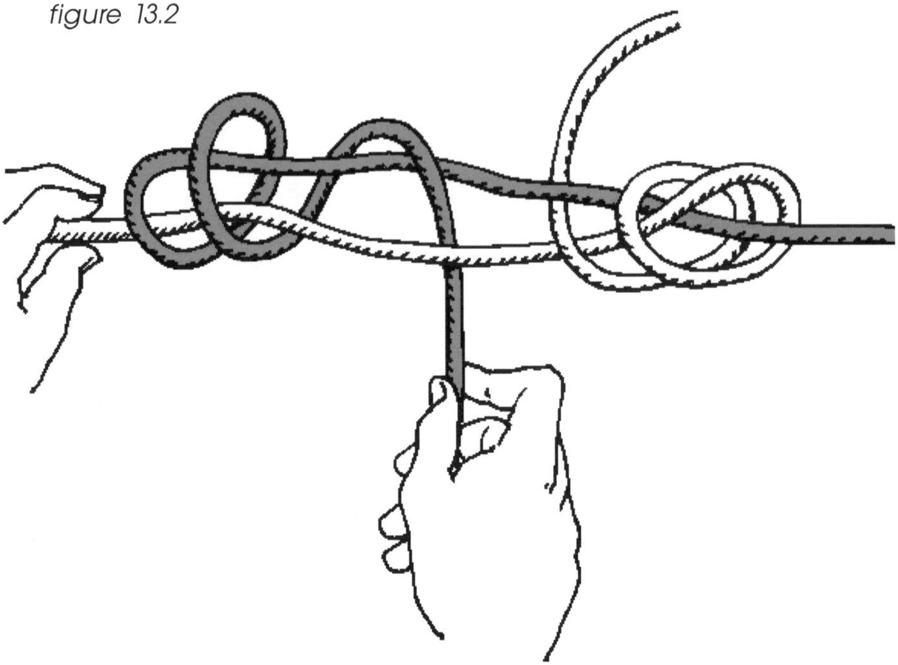

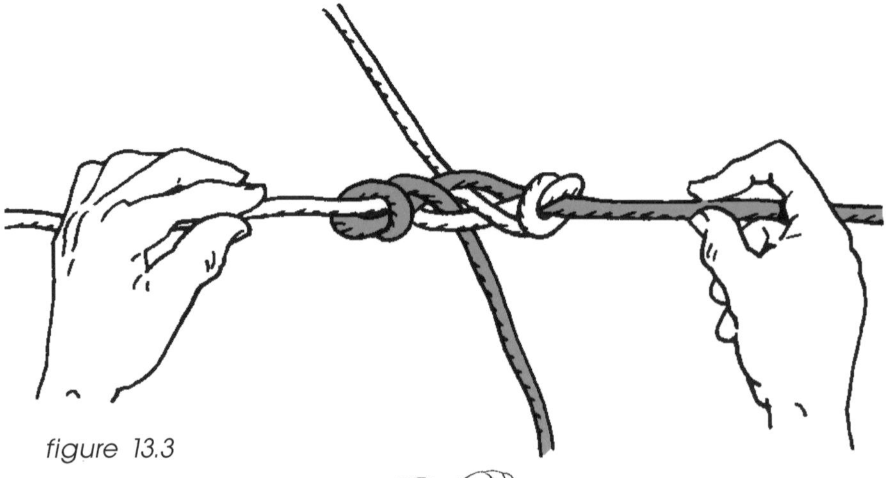

figure 13.3

between your forefinger and thumb, and with the other hand make up to five turns with the working end of the line, that extends on that hand's side, around the standing part of the other line (*figure 13.1* shows two turns). Then take the working end back towards the point of the cross and insert it on the other side of the X between the other working end and the standing part. These turns are repeated with the other working end which is then inserted through the same opening (*figure 13.2*). It is important that both ends are passed through the same opening, and that one travels from top to bottom and the other from bottom to top. The knot is then pulled tight by holding a standing part in each hand and tightening it by jerking it, which helps the turns to seat correctly (*figure 13.3*). For very low poundage line, pull steadily instead of jerking.

Bowline: one of the most useful shipboard knots, used to form a standing loop in the end of a line. The bowline is easy to tie and produces a strong, non-slip knot.

One way of tying this knot is first to form a bight and then thread the working end up

through it (*figure 14.1*). Complete the knot by passing the end around behind the standing part and back down through the bight (*figure 14.2*), and then pulling it tight.

Alternatively, and more professionally, begin by holding the standing part of the line in your left hand and with the working end in your right hand lay it across the standing part to form a bight and hold it there firmly

figure 14.1

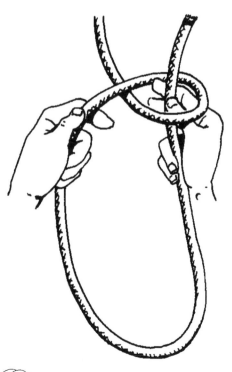

between your right forefinger and thumb. Now lift your left hand so that the bight starts to loop over the working end, meanwhile turning your right hand clockwise so that the working end turns down and inwards towards the bottom of the bight. Continue to turn the working end as the standing part loops over it and forms a second bight, so that the working end turns upwards to poke up through this second bight that you have formed (*figure 14.1*). Complete the knot as before.

figure 14.2

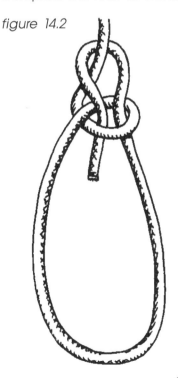

figure 15.1

Bowline on a bight: forms two loops which do not slide, most parts of the knot being made in double rope. In its early stages it is formed like a bowline, except that a bight of rope is used.

Form a bight and use this doubled rope to follow the instructions for a bowline (*see* page 21) up to *figure 14.1*. Now instead of taking the end of the bight around the

figure 15.2

figure 15.3

standing part, pull enough of the bight through the top bight (*figure 15.1*), separate it so that you can pull it down over the two lower bights (*figure 15.2*) then take it up to the back of the knot to a position around the standing parts (*figure 15.3*) and pull it tight. You now have a strong loop in the middle of a line, although its ends were not available to you.

Bowline bend: a simple yet secure way of joining any two lines together, consisting of two interlocking bowlines.

Bowse down: to draw tight a line by means of a purchase.

Braided rope *see* **plaited rope**.

Breaking strength: the estimated load, calculated by the manufacturers, that will

cause a rope to part. This is not a safe working load (*see* page 142), which takes into account other factors.

Relative breaking strengths of 12mm (0.5in) three-stranded laid ropes are as follows, when hemp is the norm:

manilla 93.5%
hemp 100%
polyethylene 144%
polypropylene 193%
polyester 219%
polyamide 300%
Kevlar (braided) 706.5%

see also knot strength, rope strength, safe working load and security.

Bucket hitch, anchor bend or **fisherman's bend:** an ideal knot for making a lanyard fast to the handle of a bucket, and so this has become most popularly known as the bucket hitch; in addition, this knot is indeed a hitch rather than a bend. It is a variation of the round turn and two half hitches and is very strong, with excellent holding properties.

First take a round turn on the anchor ring or post to which you are affixing the rope, then pass the end around behind the standing part (*figure 16.1*) and tuck it

figure 16.1

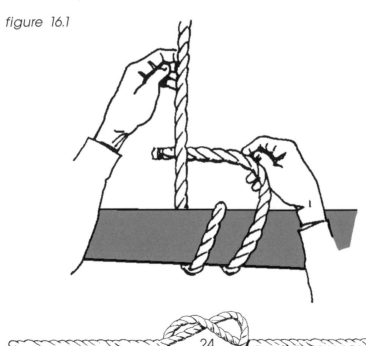

24

figure 16.2

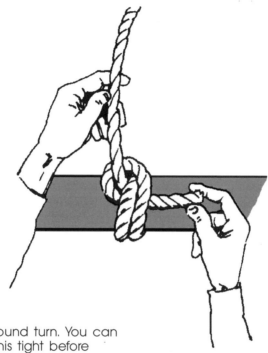

under the round turn. You can then work this tight before taking a half hitch around the standing part (*figure 16.2*). When using this knot with an anchor, seize the working end to the standing part for security, or alternatively tie a bowline on the standing part with the working end.

We recommend an alternative finish when you are using a slippery rope, similar to that which can be used for a buntline fisherman's bend (*see* page 28 *figure 19.2*), whereby after tying the standard bucket hitch you tuck back the working end into the lay of the standing part.

Bulldog grip: a metal fastening used to clamp two wires togetherside by side. It consists of a shaped part into which a U-shaped bolt fits, with the two wires trapped between. It is tightened by two nuts. The bulldog grip is not suitable for rope.

Bulldog splice: probably the simplest way of creating an eye splice in a wire rope. The rope is turned around a thimble and the end secured against the standing part with bulldog grips (*figure 17*).

figure 17

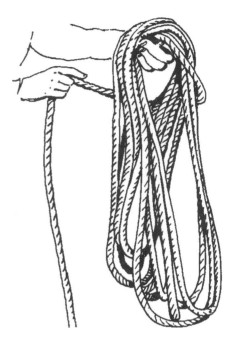

figure 18.1

Buntline coil or **gasket coil:** holds a made-up rope in position against a cleat, or when stowing a rope. Coil the rope in the usual way, and when you reach the last metre (yard) or so, wrap the end around the coils four or five times (*figure 18.1*). Next pass a bight through the upper part of the coil above the turns (*figure 18.2*), open it out and slip it forward over the top of the coil, then bring it down to lie on top of the turns (*figure 18.3*). It will then

figure 18.3

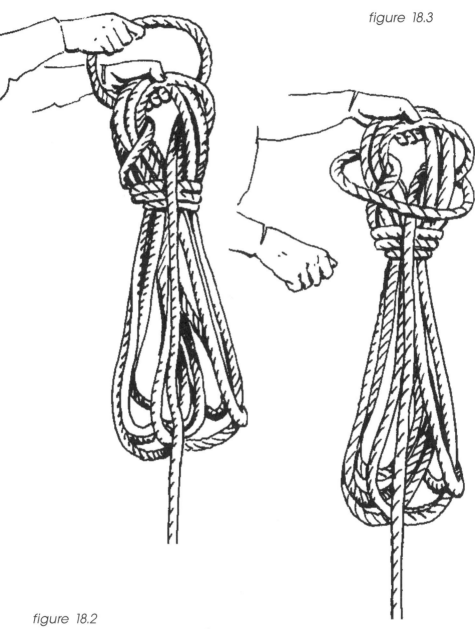

figure 18.2

lock when the slack is taken up (*figure 18.4*); to release it, simply raise the bight back over the top of the coil.

figure 18.4

Buntline fisherman's bend: secures slippery ropes when a bucket hitch or fisherman's bend is not sufficient. The knot is formed by starting with a bucket hitch (*see* page 24), to the point after the end has been worked tight and before a half hitch is made on the standing part. Take the end down around the standing part, then back across itself towards the initial round turn, before taking a second turn around the standing part in the same direction as the first. Then tuck the end up between the turns, forming a clove hitch (*figure 19.1*). The knot can then be worked tight. We recommend an alternative finish when you are using a slippery rope (*figure 19.2*), whereby after tying the standard basic hitch (*figure 19.1*) you tuck back the working end into the lay of the standing part.

Buntline hitch: originally used to secure the buntline ropes on old square riggers, but today it is most often used to knot a neck tie. Take the tie around your neck, bringing the working end, in this instance the longer (and wider) end, over the standing part before making a turn around it. Now bring the end up through the bight around your neck, and then tuck it

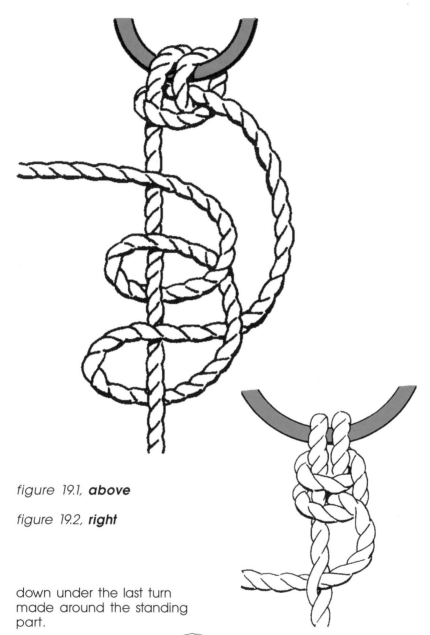

figure 19.1, **above**

figure 19.2, **right**

down under the last turn
made around the standing
part.

C

Cable: any large rope or chain.

Cable-laid: rope that comprises three hawser-laid ropes, each of three strands, twisted together left-handed to form a large nine-stranded rope.

Capsize: the loss or distortion of the characteristic layout of a knot, owing to tugging or overloading.

figure 20.1

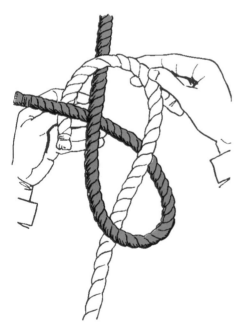

Carabiner or **karabiner:** a metal snap lock used by climbers as an attachment for ropes.

Carrick bend: although it is very useful, being strong, secure, and also readily undone, the carrick bend is not a well-known knot. In many ways it is similar to the reef knot, even to the extent that a minor error will result in a granny knot. It is a useful means of joining two ends, particularly of large ropes or ropes of slightly different sizes and materials, and even when soaking wet, it will not jam. This makes it ideal for towing lines or anchor cables, but climbers may find that it is too bulky to pass freely through a karabiner. In order to minimise this problem, the tails should be seized to their respective standing parts, as otherwise they can project at awkward angles.

Take a bight in one rope, and pass its end across beneath its standing part. Then pass the end of the other rope through this bight and then over the standing part and underneath the tail of the first rope (*figure 20.1*). Next bring it out between the first bight and its own standing part to form a second bight (*figure 20.2*), and pull the tails tight: in

figure 20.3

figure 20.2

this way, you have woven it alternately over and under each successive part.

The tails should be on opposite sides of the knot, and in really heavy ropes or particularly stiff ones can either be seized or half hitched back onto their standing parts. The bend is perfectly symmetrical, and the two bights will take up right angles to each other when under load (*figure 20.3*).

Carrick mat: with the standing part on the left, form a bight to the right taking the end back under the standing part, and make another bight underneath the first but bringing the end back over the standing part. Then reeve the end through (*figure 21.1*) from the top left to bottom right under, over, under, over; then take it under the left-hand side to meet the standing part (*figure 21.2*). You have now formed the basic pattern of the mat, and follow it around with the working end of the rope again and again (*figure 21.3*) to produce a finished mat. The more circuits you make, the larger the mat becomes.

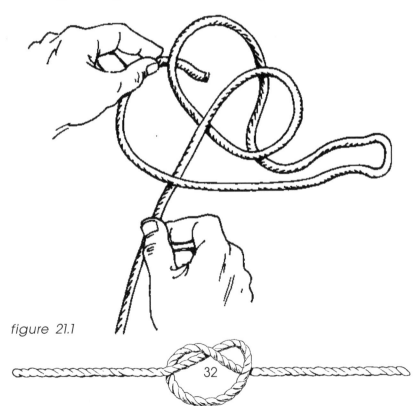

figure 21.1

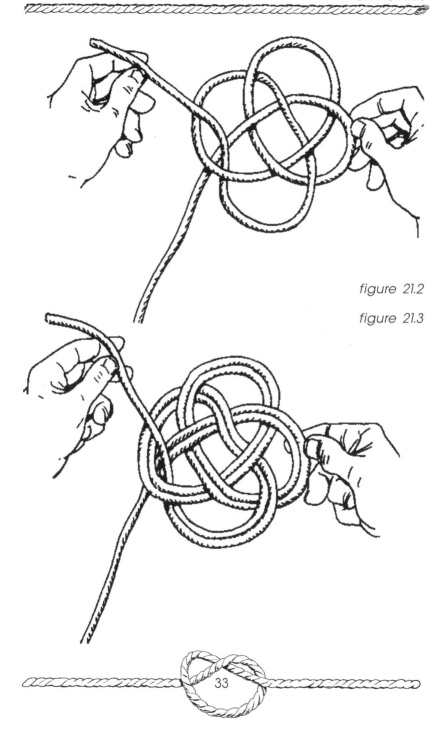

figure 21.2

figure 21.3

Cast: *see* **forming a knot**.

Cat's paw: an efficient method for hitching a sling to a hook, provided that both standing parts are under load. It prevents the rope from sliding over the hook and thus ensures an even lift.

First lay out the rope to make a bight in the sling. Fold it down over the standing parts to form two further bights.

figure 22.1, **left**

figure 22.2, **above**

Then twist these two bights once or twice outwards against their standing parts (*figure 22.1*), and slip the bights over the hook (*figure 22.2*).

Chain plait or **drummer's plait:**
begin with an overhand knot,
except that the lower part
should be a bight, not an end
(*figure 23.1*). Thereafter it is
purely a matter of creating a
bight through a bight (*figure
23.2*); to finish the plait, reeve
the end through the last bight
(*figure 23.3*).

figure 23.1

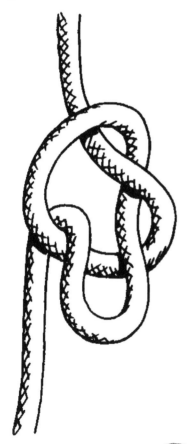

figure 23.2

Chain splice: joins a rope to a
normal small link in a chain,
enabling the whole to pass
through a naval pipe.

Unlay one strand for about six
or seven turns and set it aside.
Reeve the remaining two
strands through the end link
of the chain and back to the

point at which the single strand has been unlaid. Then unlay the two strands back towards the chain, leaving only enough laid rope to form the eye itself. Now unlay the first strand for a further six or seven turns (*figure 24*) and replace it in the rope by one of the other two strands, just as in a long splice (*see* page 111) until the second strand reaches the point to which the first strand is unlaid. Cut the remaining unlaid strand at a length that allows it to be tucked, one over and one under, against the lay for four or five times, working around the rope. Now cut the first strand to the same length as the unlaid end of the second strand, and tuck away both of these strands.

figure 23.3, **above**

figure 24, **below**

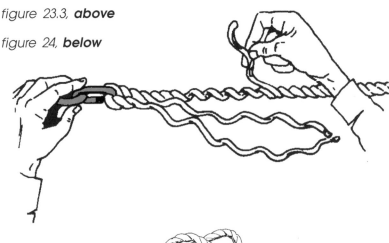

36

figure 25.1

Chair knot or **man harness:** suitable, as the name suggests, for lowering an injured person over the side of a ship.

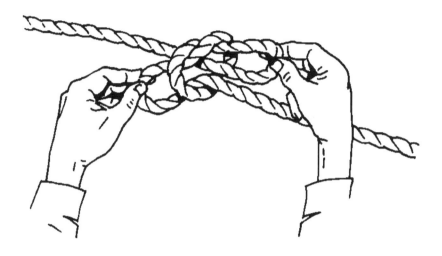

figure 25.2

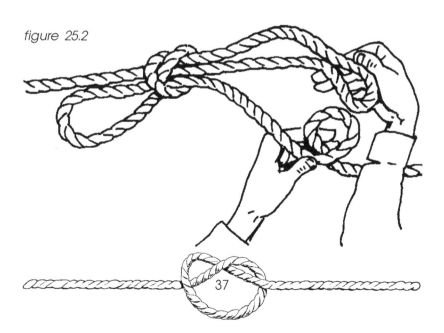

figure 25.3

The rope must be at least twice as long as the distance of the descent to be made. Form a Tom Fool's knot (*see* page 173) with very large bights in the centre of this rope, so that the smaller bight will fit the casualty around the body and under the armpits and the larger bight is twice this size, for the person to sit in. Form a half hitch in the standing part below each of the two bights in the Tom Fool's knot (*figure 25.1*) and cast each half hitch over the end of its corresponding bight (*figure 25.2*, in which the bights are shown much smaller for the sake of displaying the knot), pulling each half hitch snugly up to the centre of the knot (*figure 25.3*). Then fit this harness to

the casualty, with the larger bight under the thighs to position the knot in front of the casualty. This should prevent overbalancing during the lowering process, with the knot immediately above the casualty's chest level supporting the weight. Throw the half of the rope from the small bight around the casualty's torso down to an assistant, and run the other half of the rope over a strong support such as a railing. The assistant below hauls off with his standing part to guide the descent, while you feed the upper half over the support to take the strain as the casualty is lowered.

Cleating *see* **belaying a rope with a cleat**.

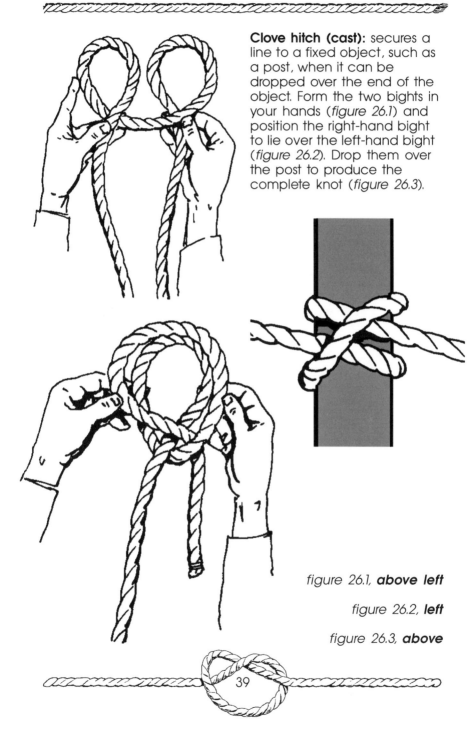

Clove hitch (cast): secures a line to a fixed object, such as a post, when it can be dropped over the end of the object. Form the two bights in your hands (*figure 26.1*) and position the right-hand bight to lie over the left-hand bight (*figure 26.2*). Drop them over the post to produce the complete knot (*figure 26.3*).

figure 26.1, **above left**

figure 26.2, **left**

figure 26.3, **above**

Clove hitch (turned): used to secure a line to a fixed continuous object such as a railing, when a load is applied to both sides of the knot. If a load is applied to only one side the knot will slip.

First take a turn around the object to be secured, with the end positioned under the standing part. Put a half hitch on above this turn, by passing the end around behind the post and tucking it back under itself (*figure 27.1*) in front of the post. Then pull tight the knot (*figure 27.2*).

figure 27.1

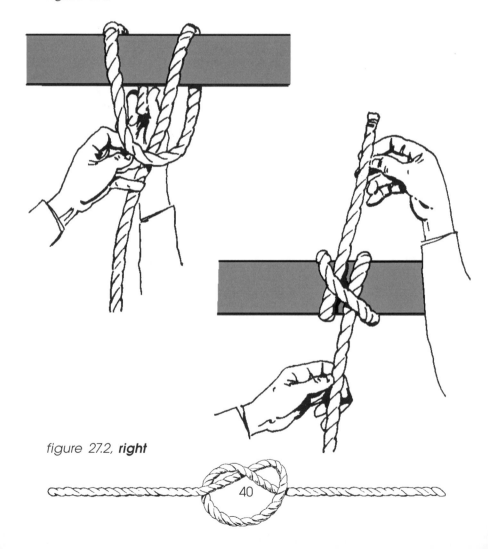

figure 27.2, **right**

Coach whipping: covers rails and is worked with an even number of strands.

Seize the strands at one end of the rail and distribute them evenly around its circumference. Split the strands into two equal groups

figure 28

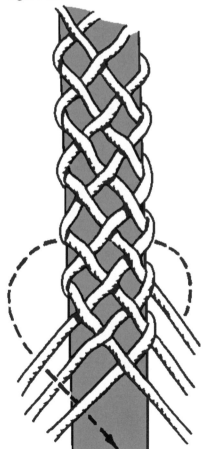

and interweave them around the rail by taking the top strand on one side back under the rail and then weaving it under, over, under, over (depending on the number of strands employed) through the strands on the other side, finally passing the working strand over the rail back to its own side. Then work the top strand on the other side in the same fashion, then the top strand from the first side, alternating until the area to be covered is completed (*figure 28*). Finish off as you began by whipping the ends to the rail.

Cockscombing (single-stranded): this is an ideal way of covering a circular object, because the gaps that naturally occur on the inside are taken up by the curvature of the object. Cockscombing is comprised quite simply, of alternate hitches worked backwards and forwards.

Start by forming a cow hitch (*figure 29.1*) then, working in one direction only, continue to make hitches forwards (*figure 29.2*) then follow this with a hitch backwards. As you work around the ring, the gaps that would form on the inside of a straight cylindrical object close together within the circle (*figure 29.3*).

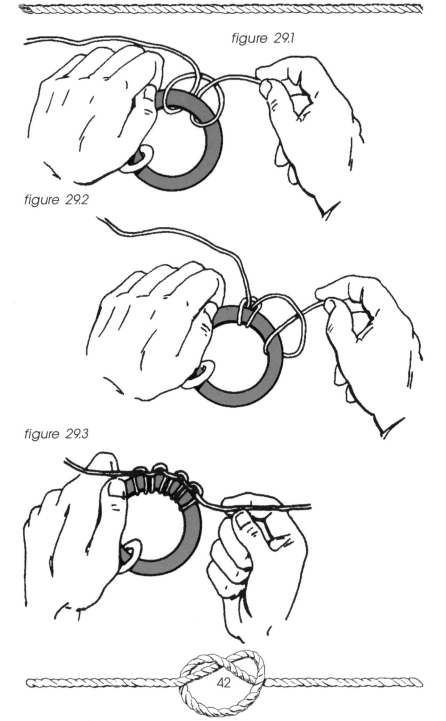

figure 29.1

figure 29.2

figure 29.3

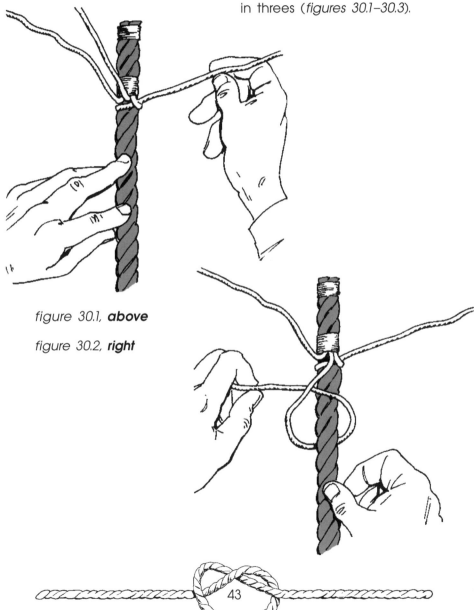

Cockscombing (three-stranded): in the three- stranded running cockscomb, the difference is that the half hitches are made alternately clockwise and anticlockwise in threes (*figures 30.1–30.3*).

figure 30.1, **above**

figure 30.2, **right**

figure 30.3

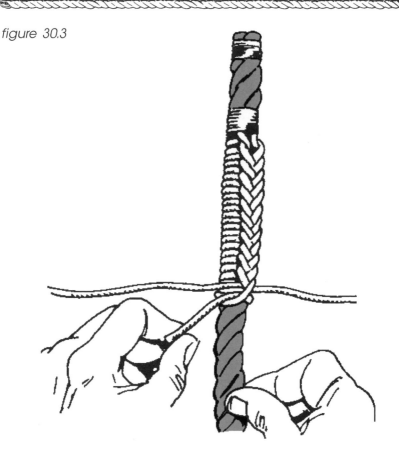

Coiling: it is important to coil a rope down properly, as this not only affords easier use when it is next required, but also avoids kinks and takes up less space, which is often at a premium aboard ship.

Coiling a heaving line: which must fly out well when thrown, so take care to ensure that there are an absolute minimum of kinks or crossed turns. You should coil the heaving line with each bight smaller than the previous one, so that it will not catch.

A heaving line being coiled on the deck is shown in *figure 31.1*, and *figure 31.2* shows it being coiled in the hand.

figure 31.1

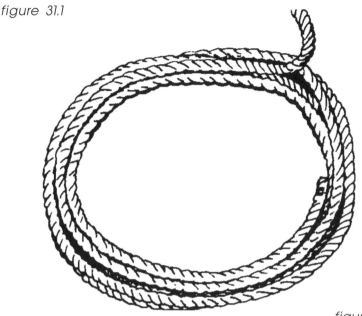

figure 31.2

Coiling a rope with a bight: as an untidy or uncoiled rope can be extremely dangerous on board a boat, or to keep a rope coiled tightly for hanging up in storage, you should form a bight in the last coil and tuck it through the previous coil to provide an ideal solution. However, do remember that a bight in a mooring rope must be long enough to pass over a samson post or bollard.

Another method, possibly the simplest way of keeping loose lines (especially those hanging from cleats) tidy, is to make a

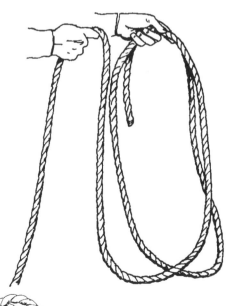

figure 31.3

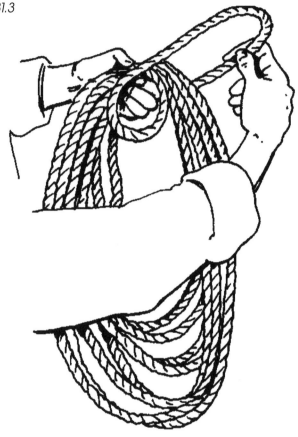

coil starting close to the cleat. Then, holding the coil in your left hand, pass the right hand through the middle of the coil, taking hold of the rope near to where it leaves the cleat. Pull the rope through and twist it (*figure 31.3*), thereby forming a **coil with a half hitch**. Now place the loop that has been formed over the upper horn of the cleat.

When making a coil in a rope with a fixed end, always work towards the other end, as this will avoid kinks.

Common sennit (three-stranded): the simplest of the sennits, the common sennit is useful when mat-making using long lengths.

Arrange the strands with two to the right and one to the left. Start by taking the outside right strand across the inside right strand to the middle. Then move the left side strand across the strand that became the new inside right strand, to the middle. Now take the strand that has become the new outside right strand across the inside right strand to the middle (*figure 32.1*). This completes the first full sequence of movements, so that you can repeat the process until you reach your required length of sennit (*figure 32.2*).

figure 32.1

figure 32.2

Common sennit (seven-stranded): a more complex but more pleasing version of the three-stranded common sennit, to which the same principles apply.

Arrange the strands with four to the right and three to the left. Start by taking the outside right strand over the other three right-hand side strands to the centre. Now, because of the way it is laid across, it has become the inside left-hand strand. Now take the outside left strand, pass it over the (now three) other left-hand strands to the centre,

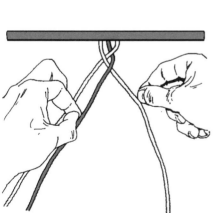

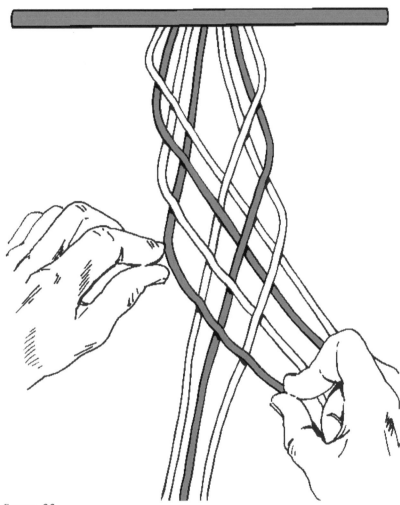

figure 33

where it becomes the new inside right-hand side strand. Repeat the these actions with the new outside right strand, then the new outside left strand, until all strands have been moved once (*figure 33*). As with other sennits, this sequence of workings can be repeated until the required length of the sennit is obtained.

Common whipping: is an adequate whipping in most instances, and quite simple to carry out. In order to ensure a smooth finish, you can apply a little beeswax to the twine prior to whipping.

Begin by laying one end of the whipping twine, which can be used directly from the spool, along the rope. Then take turns tightly around the rope (*figure 34.1*), thereby anchoring the end. The turns can be taken around the rope either towards you, or away from you, when applying the whipping. Leave the last few turns loose, with

figure 34.1

figure 34.2

the working end of the twine threaded underneath them. Then work tight these final turns, as you draw down the end and finally cut it close. The length of the finished whipping should be about one and a half times the rope's diameter (*figure 34.2*).

Constrictor knot: a modern knot that will grip tightly and stay tied. It is most useful for securing the neck of a bag or sack, or can be used as temporary whipping, as we have shown it.

Take a round turn around the rope with the working end, then across the standing end, and form another round turn. Then bring the working end

figure 35.1

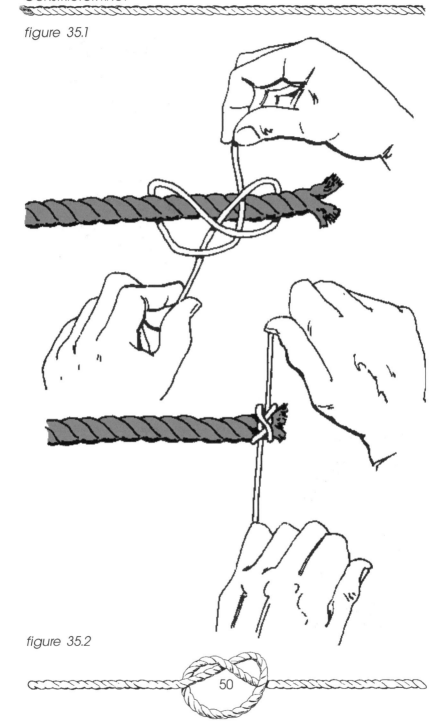

figure 35.2

over the top of the standing end again, before tucking it up under the bight of the round turn, at which point (*figure 35.1*) the knot is loosely tied. You can then pull the knot tighter, to the tension you need (*figure 35.2*). It is worth remembering that you should use a hard cord when the item being tied is soft and yielding so that the cord will bite, and *vice versa*; use a soft cord for a hard object, in order to obtain the best grip.

There are other methods you can use for tying this knot, but this method is suitable for all situations.

Continuous crowning: provides a decorative alternative for covering cylindrical objects. It is created by forming one crown on top of another, with any number of strands; *see also* crown knot, crown plait (spiral and straight) and wall and crown plait.

Continuous diamond knotting *see* **diamond plait**.

Continuous figure of eight: the figure of eight is extensively used as the seaman's stopper knot. However, where there is a continuous requirement for them, for example in a lifeline where they enable easier climbing down, it would be exhausting work to pull 15m or 20m (16 or 22 yds) of standing part through each knot. There is an easier way of forming continuous figures of eight in one movement, and this is shown here on a small scale (*figures 36.1–36.3*).

figure 36.1

figure 36.2, **above**

figure 36.3, **below**

Form a bight in the rope, and twist it to form another bight above the first. You can repeat this as many times as required (*figure 36.1*). When you have reached the appropriate number, or you run out of rope, pass the working end through the top bights in the figures of eight

that you have formed (*figure 36.2*). As you continue to pull the working end through, a continuous line of figures of eight will form (*figure 36.3*). The distance between the figures of eight is governed by the length of the lower bights; *see also* figure of eight.

Continuous walling: a continuous formation of wall knots can be made on any number of strands, but only around a cylindrical object.

Start by evenly spacing and then whipping the strands around the object, and then form wall knots (*see* page 187), one on top of another, until the required length is reached; *see also* double wall, wall and crown knot, wall and crown plait, wall knot, and wall plait.

Contline *see* **cantline**.

Cord: generally used to describe all line, of any material or of any size, which does not have a dedicated purpose. However, strictly speaking, it is a small line under 10mm (0.4in) diameter, and comprised of several tightly twisted yarns.

Core *see* **heart**.

Cow hitch or **lark's head:** when formed intentionally, the cow hitch is used to secure a line with equal strain at both ends, which must lie in the same direction, to a ring or spar. However, the hitch is often arrived at unintentionally when trying to form a round turn and two half hitches, and the second

figure 37

half hitch is wrongly formed in the opposite direction to the first.

To form the cow hitch, take a turn around the ring, and pass the end over the standing

part. Then take a second turn, but in the opposite direction to the first, and tuck the end under itself,thereby forming a second standing part. The completed knot is shown in *figure 37*.

An alternative method of tying the knot which is both simpler and easier, is to make a bight in the rope, push this through the ring, then pass the two ends through the bight. Unfortunately it is not always possible to tie the knot this way.

Cow hitch and toggle: an improvisation to the cow hitch, used when the two standing ends are fixed and only the bight is available for tying the knot.

Pass a bight of rope through the ring to form this knot; insert a rod (a marline spike is ideal) under the standing parts and over the bight (*figure 38*). The knot will be perfectly secure, provided there is equal strain on both ends.

Crawford knot: an excellent way of tying monofilament line to a hook, being both easy to tie and with a good knot strength.

To form it, pass the working end through the eye of the hook and draw through about 20cm (8in) of line. Pass the working end behind the standing part, then back in front of the standing part and down towards the eye of the hook, taking it around both

figure 38

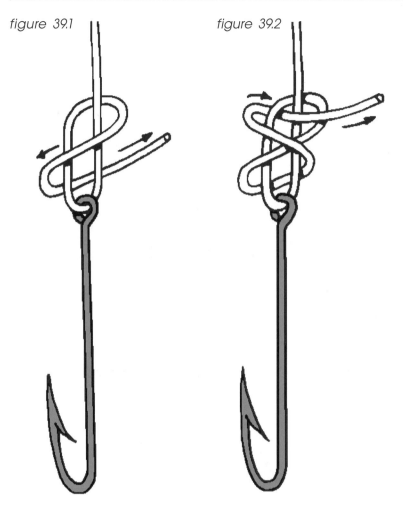

figure 39.1

figure 39.2

sides of the loop (*figure 39.1*), back across the front and up towards the top bight, thereby forming a figure eight. Now tuck the end through the top of the bight and the standing part (*figure 39.2*). To draw tight the knot, hold the bight just above the eye of the hook, and pull on the working end. Now pull on the standing part and the knot will slide down to the hook eye and you can trim off the end.

Cringles: are eyes formed in a bolt rope or sail edge, and used for sail handling lines.

figure 40.1

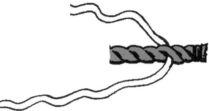

To make them, take a length of single strand about six times the circumference of the cringle you want to form. Pass

figure 40.2

the strand under one or two strands of the rope, and pull through one third of it (*figure 40.1*). Take the shorter of the projecting ends of the single strand around the rope and then wrap it three times around its longer end (*figure 40.2*). Working with the longer end of the single strand, pass it through one or two strands of the rope (*figure 40.3*), around the back of the rope and then work it back towards the right-hand side, where you can thread it through one or two strands of the rope (*figure 40.4*). You can now splice the two ends of the single strand into the rope (*figure 40.5*) and trim off any excess.

figure 40.3

figure 40.4

figure 40.5

Crowning *see* **continuous crowning**.

Crown knot: forms the basis of many stopper knots, but it cannot be used alone, as it will come undone.

Unlay the rope to the required length, and then interweave the strands. You can use any number of strands. Work with the lay of the rope, by passing each strand around over its neighbour and the last strand and down through the bight of the first (*figure 41*). All of the strands will emerge

from the bottom of the knot (unlike the otherwise similar wall knot, where the strands emerge from the top) and be pointing downwards. The knot can now be pulled tight; *see also* back splice, continuous crowning, crown plait, double crown, wall knot and wall and crown plait.

Crown plait, spiral: created by continuous crowning with not more than four strands, in an anticlockwise direction and without a central heart. The result will be a spiral effect – *figure 42.1* shows the view

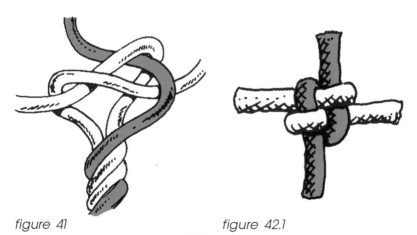

figure 41

figure 42.1

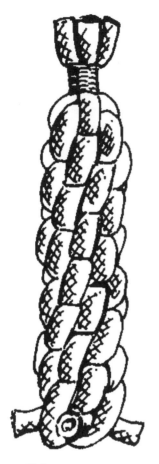

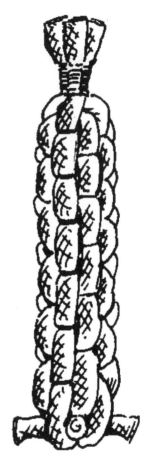

figure 42.2

figure 43

from underneath, and *figure 42.2* shows a completed plait; *see also* continuous crowning and crown knot.

Crown plait, straight: an alternative to the spiral crown plait, formed by making alternate clockwise and anticlockwise crowns. A chain-like pattern is the result (*figure 43*). The crown plait is often used to form fenders and toggles, and the ends can be either whipped, or finished with a single wall knot followed by a decorative knot.

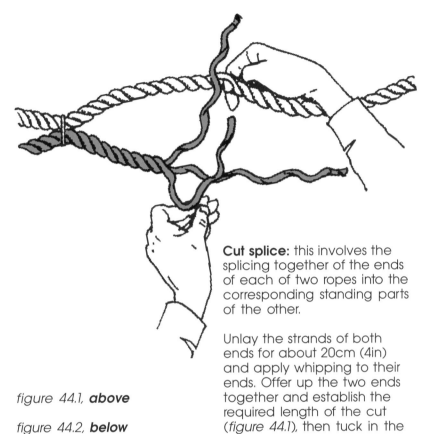

Cut splice: this involves the splicing together of the ends of each of two ropes into the corresponding standing parts of the other.

Unlay the strands of both ends for about 20cm (4in) and apply whipping to their ends. Offer up the two ends together and establish the required length of the cut (*figure 44.1*), then tuck in the

figure 44.1, **above**

figure 44.2, **below**

same way as for an eye splice, by taking the central strand and tucking it under any strand of the standing part of the second rope, against the lay. Then tuck the left-hand strand, passing it to the left of the first strand, over the strand of the standing part under which the first strand has been tucked, and under the next strand of the standing part. Then take the third strand around the other side of the standing part and tuck it back under the remaining strand of the standing part. This completes the full tuck. Now continue to

tuck over one, under one with the three strands, against the lay, until you have completed three full tucks (*figure 44.2*). You can now cut the tails and repeat the process, with the right-hand end being spliced into the left-hand standing part.

D

Dacron *see* **polyester**.

Decorative shamrock knot: looks the same both front and back, and despite looking decorative has very little practical use.

figure 45.1

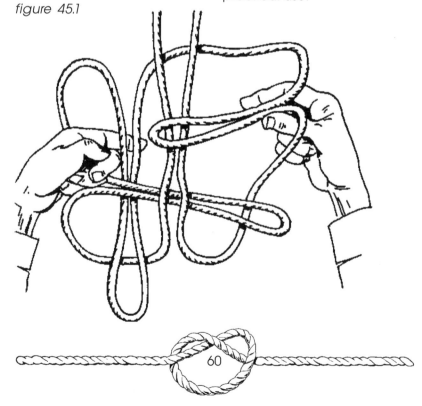

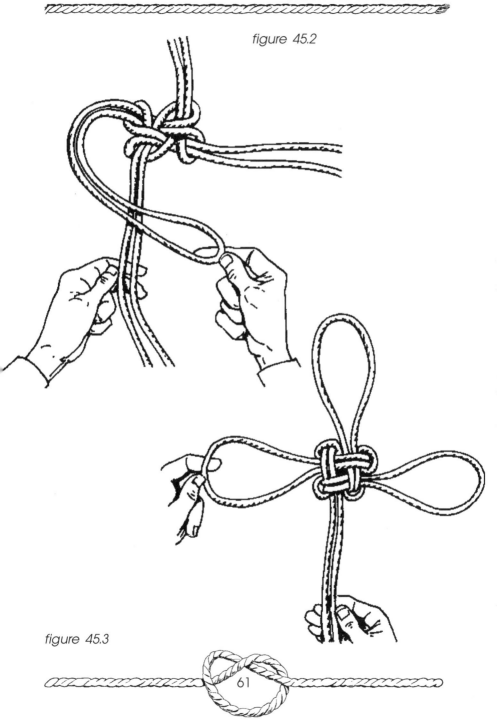

figure 45.2

figure 45.3

Form a circle in the rope, with the two ends both coming towards you. Now take the two ends together, up and away from you over the circle, to point to the top. Form a bight in the lower left side of the circle, and pass this under the two ends to lie above the lower right-hand side of the circle. Next, form a bight in the top left-hand side of the circle and pass it under the first bight. Then make a bight in the top right-hand side of the circle, and pass it over the two ends and under the top left-hand bight (*figure 45.1*). This completes the first stage, which can be pulled tight.

To complete the knot, pull down the top left-hand bight over the bottom left-hand bight (*figure 45.2*), to form a loop at the left.Then take the bottom left bight over the top left-hand bight and over the bottom right-hand bight. Continue this process by taking the bottom right-hand bight over the bottom left-hand bight and over the top right-hand bight. Then take the ends from the top right-hand side over the bottom right-hand bight and tuck them into the loop formed at the left side. You can now pull all the bights tight to complete the knot (*figure 45.3*).

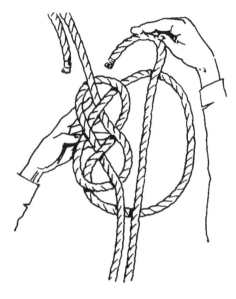

figure 46.1, **above**

figure 46.2, **below**

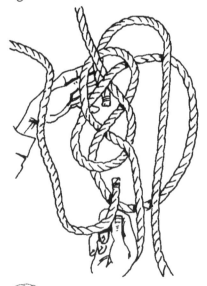

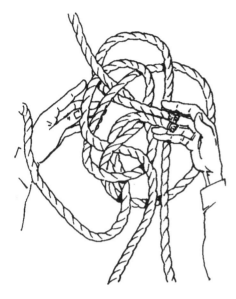

figure 46.3, **above**

figure 46.4, **below**

Diamond hitching *see* **diamond plait**.

Diamond knot: a decorative stopper knot, developed from the carrick bend (*see* page 30), which has been formed in the centre of a rope with a small bight. This small bight eventually forms the eye of the knot.

Make an overhand loop and take the working end on to make a larger bight to the right, before laying this underneath the first bight. Take the working end over the top of the larger bight just formed, and around behind the standing part, before bringing the working end back down over the right-hand side of the first, smaller, bight. Tuck it in and out of that bight so as to weave it under the right-hand side of the large loop. Now take the working end to the top of the knot (*figure 46.1*) and pass it down behind the knot and up through the centre, while tucking the standing end down into the bottom of the large loop, up behind the rest of the knot (*figure 46.2*) and back up through the eye of the carrick bend together with the working end (*figure 46.3*). Then work the knot towards the eye and draw tight all parts (*figure 46.4*).

Diamond knot, on four strands: holding the four strands in your left hand, form a bight in each and hold them secure between your thumb and forefinger. Then take each strand anticlockwise past its adjacent bight and up through the next (*figures 47.1– 47.3*) and pull all working ends together to form the finished knot.

figure 47.1

Diamond plait, diamond hitching or **continuous diamond knotting:** can be used to form a covering for any cylindrical object. It is comprised of one diamond knot on top of another. The plait can be formed by including both single and double diamond knots, and a tighter effect created by making crowns between the diamonds; *see also* diamond knot.

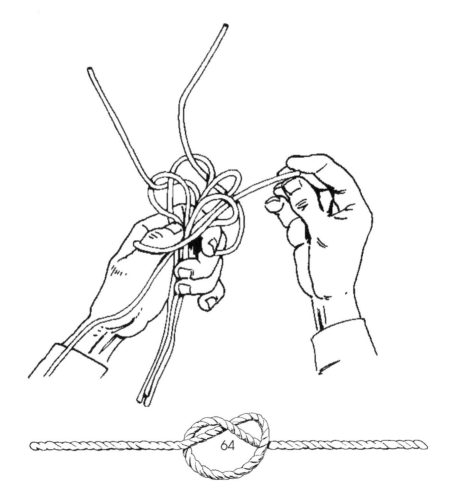

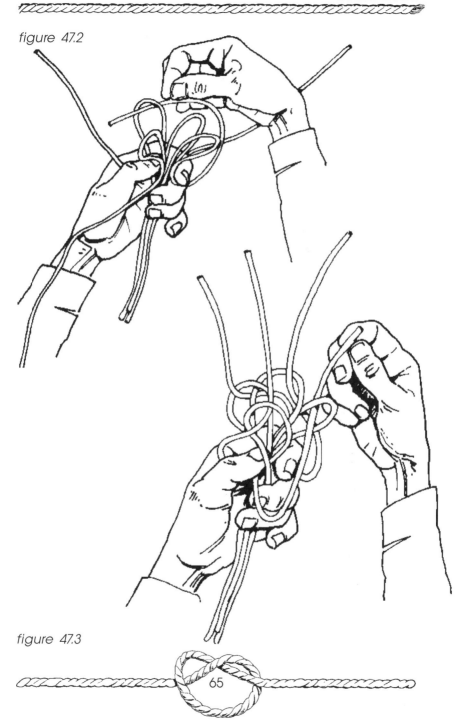

figure 47.2

figure 47.3

Dog: the act of winding the working end of a rope back several times around itself, or another larger rope. This is done with the lay, and has the effect of securing the rope temporarily against a lengthwise pull.

Double becket bend *see* **double sheet bend**.

figure 48

Double carrick bend: used to join two lengths of rope, but only holds securely when the ends are stopped to their standing parts, otherwise the knot will turn and can work loose. It has an added advantage in that it can be formed where one end has already been secured, spliced or seized to its standing part.

Make it by forming a bight in one end, or twist the eye in the rope with the secured end. Take the second rope behind the end loop and up, at the top of the crossover point, to take it between the end and the standing part of the first rope. Now continue to work the second rope up at the lower side of the crossing point, to tuck it into the eye behind itself, and out of the eye (this is where it differs from the carrick bend) to lie against its standing part (*figure 48*), where you can secure it.

Double carrick bend sennit: an ideal way of forming a belt or strap, especially effective when two differently coloured cords are used.

First seize the two cords together, but if making a belt remember to leave sufficient cord to make a loop through

figure 49

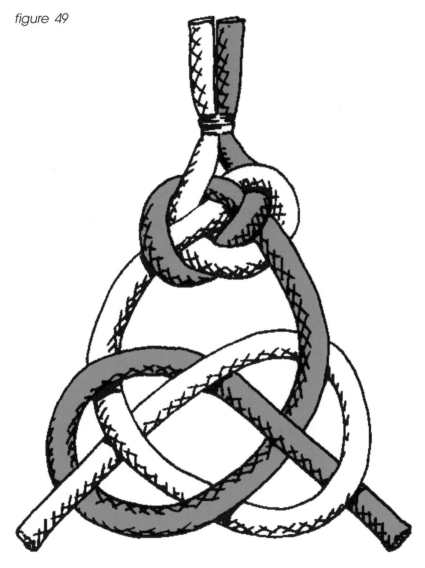

which a knob at the other
end of the belt can pass, in
order to fasten it. Then form a
series of alternating carrick
bends (*see* page 30), the first
being made with the red cord
above the white, the second
with the white above the red

(*figure 49*). After each hitch has been formed, it should be drawn tight. Continue alternating in this fashion until reaching the length of strap that you want, at which point the ends can be seized together and a knob formed if you want one as a fastening.

Double chain plait: is formed by creating a series of figure-of-eight knots which are all interwoven.

Do this by making a figure of

figure 50

eight knot (*see* page 80), then continue by taking the working end (which is the lower end in our illustration) to form a bight, the lower circle of a figure of eight, up through the top circle of the first figure of eight to link it together, and continuing around the back to form another bight. Bring the working end down across the crossover point of the eight and in through the second bottom bight (*figure 50*). Repeat this sequence until you reach the desired length. The tension of the plait can be adjusted to suit your purpose. Long mats can be formed in this way, or it is possible to make a circular mat by tightening the lower bights and opening out the top.

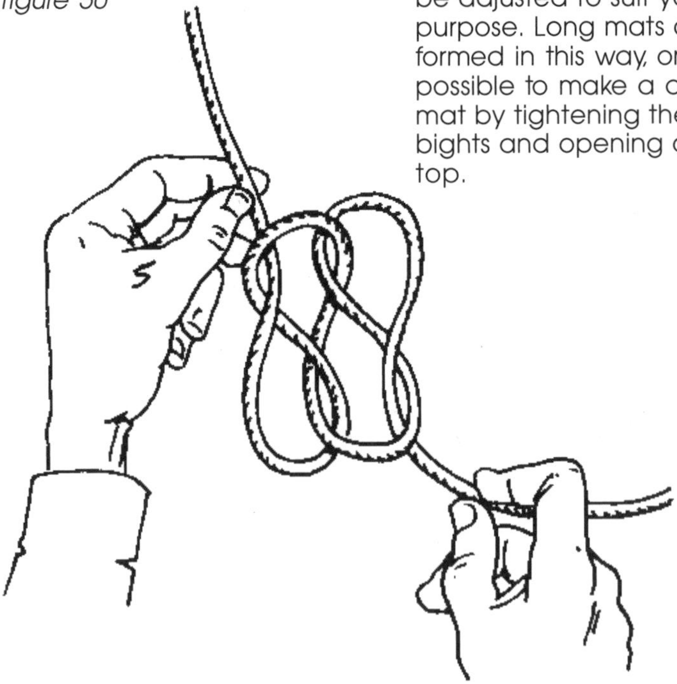

Double crown: working from an unlaid end of rope (*see* crown knot, page 57) or from a number of strands (we have used four in our illustration), pass each strand around over its anticlockwise neighbour (you can also work clockwise) with the last strand passing down through the bight of the first strand to have been worked (*figure 51.1*). This can now be pulled tight, which will have the effect of making each strand point downwards. Now pull back any one strand and make a clockwise turn around the strand it originally passed over, and this will return the strand to its original position. Repeat this with the other strands, passing the last through the now-double bight of the first (*figure 51.2*).

figure 51.1

figure 51.2

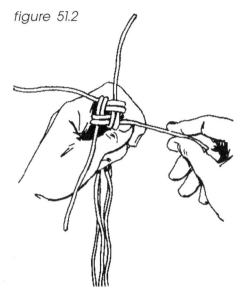

Double diamond knot: working from the diamond knot on four strands (*see* page 64), follow around with each strand by passing it under two parts and up through the third; however, the last strand will have to be taken under two double parts. All strands will again emerge at the top.

Double figure of eight: is used when a single figure of eight is not big enough to stop the rope running through an eye. It is formed in the same way as a figure of eight knot (*see* page 80), but with an extra turn taken around the standing part, before tucking the end down through the bight.

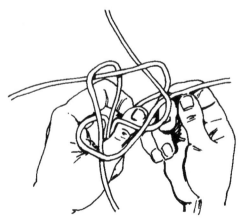

Double fisherman's knot: this is a stronger version of the fisherman's knot (*see* page 83), and particularly useful when working with a slippery material such as nylon.

Start as for the fisherman's knot, but tie a thumb knot (*see* page 171) with an extra turn in each end (*figure 52.1*), before pulling tight (*figure 52.2*) to form the completed knot.

Double line loop *see* **Bimini twist**

Double sheet bend or **double becket bend:** is more secure than the single sheet bend (*see* page 149), and preferable when one of the ropes is slippery.

Start by forming the single sheet bend, but complete a full round turn about the neck of the bight in the larger rope, before proceeding to tuck the end; you should ensure that the ends of both ropes emerge on the same side. The completed knot is illustrated in figure 53.

figure 52.1

figure 52.2

standing part five times, before passing it through the turns (*figure 54*) on the outside of the ring.

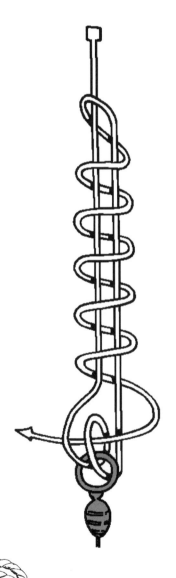

figure 53, **above**

figure 54, **right**

Double stevedore knot: a helpful knot for anglers to remember, when using gut or nylon and needing that little extra bit of knot strength.

Take the line around the ring twice: this is what provides the additional strength. Then take back the line along its standing part, twisting it around both itself and its

Double thumb knot *see* **fisherman's knot**.

Double wall: this is illustrated using four strands, held firmly in the left hand with the ends having been formed, working anticlockwise, into a wall knot (*figure 55.1; see also* page 187). However, any number of strands can be used, and it can also be formed by working clockwise. The emerging strands, which would face upwards in all wall knots, are laid alongside previous bights, which are followed around until they

emerge separately pointing upwards (*figure 55.2* has been drawn showing this flat, for clarity, but the strands should be pulled upwards).

Draw hitch or **thief knot:** provides a quick release simply by tugging at the working end. It can, however, prove disastrous. Whereas it is a perfectly efficient knot when being used as a lifeline, it is essential that the standing part, which is capable of supporting a load – the escaping thief – is not confused with the working

figure 55.1

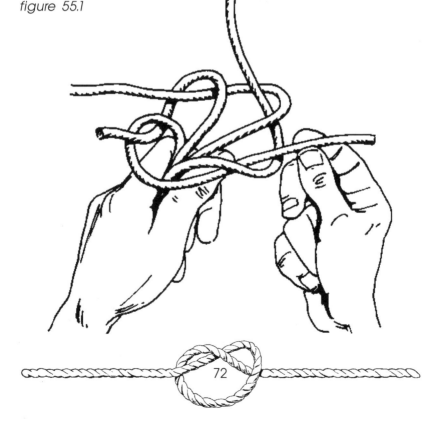

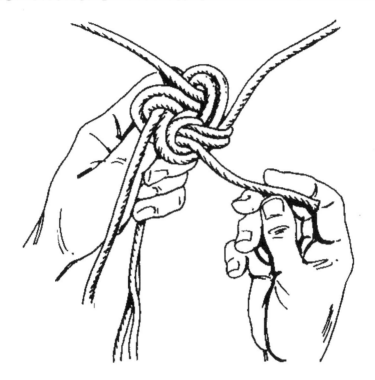

figure 55.2

end. Therefore when this knot is being used, as it is by the fire services, as a lifeline or as a means of escape, extra care must be taken to identify that end (the standing part) which can support a load.

To make it, form a bight in the rope and take this up behind the beam or loadbearing arm, and bring it down in front of the beam. Pull the standing part through the bight to form a second bight (figure 56.1), through which you pull the working end to form a third bight (figure 56.2). If you then pull down tight the standing part, which is the left-hand hanging end in our illustration, this will support a load. However as figure 56.2 also clearly illustrates, the right-hand side end will not; any load applied to that end will simply pull the rope through, thus releasing the knot.

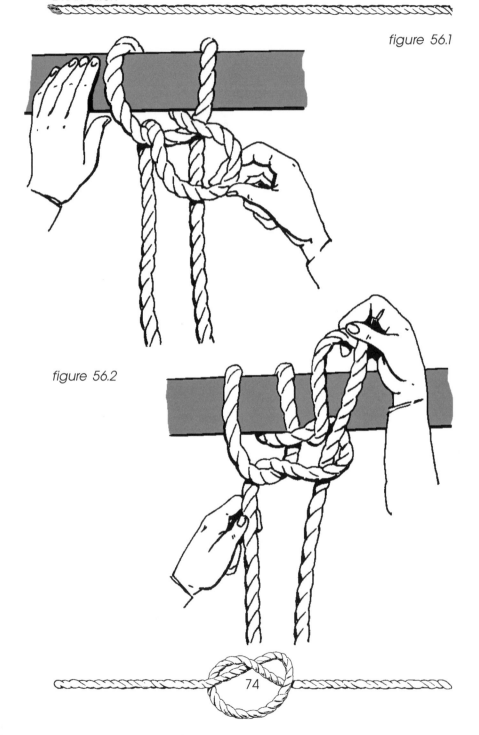

figure 56.1

figure 56.2

Drummer's plait *see* **chain plait**.

Duncan loop: this is a sliding loop that allows the lure to have action in the water, but slides down and tightens under pressure from a fish.

Form the loop by passing the line through the eye of the hook to make a bight of about 20cm (8in) for the tying of the knot. Turn about half of the working end down back towards the hook, thus forming a second bight, then take the end up and take five turns (*figure 57.1*) around both sides of the first bight. Make sure that the working end passes through the second bight (*figure 57.2*).

To tighten the knot, hold the hook with a pair of pliers and pull steadily on the working end until the loop and knot begin to tighten. Under normal pressure the knot will be secure and not slide, but when fighting a fish the loop will slide down and tighten against the eye. You can reopen the loop with your fingers for further use.

figure 57.1

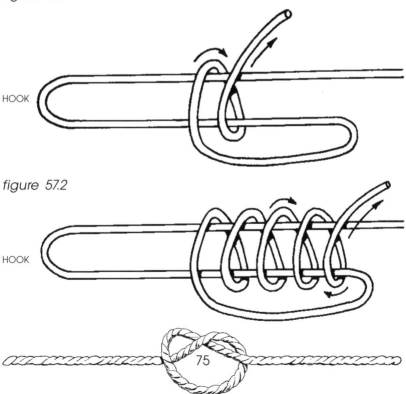

HOOK

figure 57.2

HOOK

E

Eight plait: a large rope comprised of four pairs of strands, of which two spiral clockwise and two anticlockwise, producing a strong rope that will not kink.

End: usually refers to the end of a line which is being knotted or whipped; also known as the running end or working end (*figure 58*).

figure 58

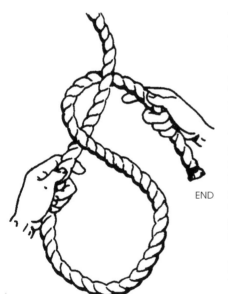

END

Englishman's knot *see* **fisherman's knot**.

English sennit (seven-stranded): this is made with four or more strands. We have illustrated the seven-stranded English sennit, which best clarifies the method of forming.

The strands should all be secured at the top, thus leaving both your hands free to form the sennit. The strands can be arranged evenly spaced to enable ease of working, and closed together prior to tightening to arrive at the finished sennit.

Working always with the strand that is on the right outside, weave the first strand under one, over one until it emerges on the left side, where it should be laid parallel to the other strands. Now take the second strand, which has become the far right strand, and weave that under one, over one to the left side. This step is now repeated until you arrive at the required length (*figure 59* shows all seven strands having been worked once).

Eye: a loop, usually made in the end of a rope by splicing it.

Eye splice (three-stranded): this is a way of forming a permanent loop in the end of a rope.

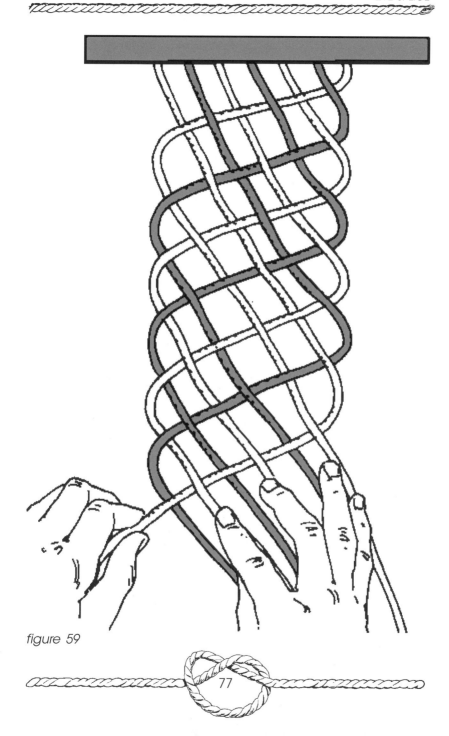

figure 59

Unlay the end of the rope just a short way, and seal the ends of the strands. This makes them easier to tuck, and also stops them from fraying. Take the middle strand and tuck it under one strand of the standing part against the lay, at a point that provides you with a loop of the required size. Then take the strand that is lying on the inside, and tuck it under the next strand of the standing part at the same point along the rope (*figure 60.1*). It is now easier to turn over the work to tuck the third strand under

the remaining strand of the standing part, at the same position as the first two strands have been tucked. In order to do this, you will have to turn this strand back upon itself so that it too is tucked into the standing part against the lay.

Working always against the lay, tuck each strand at least three times over one strand and under the next. Excess ends can be cut off (*figure 60.2*) and the finished splice rolled under the sole of the shoe to help the splice settle.

figure 60.1

figure 60.2

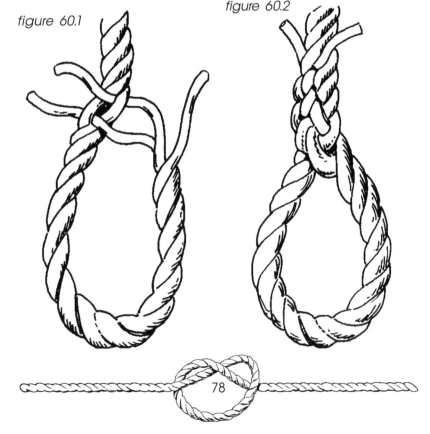

Eye splice (in the middle of a rope): this is formed in a similar way to the eye splice at the end of a rope, except that in this instance the rope is deliberately forced against its lay by twisting it in opposite directions (*figure 61.1*). Make a bight to the size of the required eye in the standing part, and use the three untwisted laid bights to tuck into the standing part to make a normal eye splice (*see* page 76). The first tuck is shown in *figure 61.2*.

figure 61.1

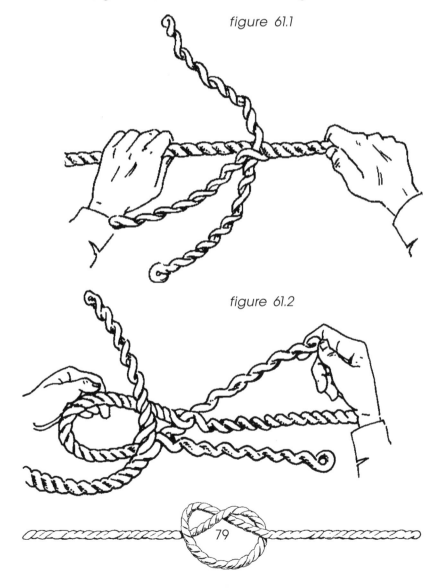

figure 61.2

figure 61.3

Remember to tuck against the lay and as described for the eye splice; three full tucks at least are required to provide sufficient strength in the eye (*figure 61.3*). Do not trim off the ends.

Fibres: the smallest element of rope construction. The fibres are twisted together to form the yarns. They are the thread-like natural vegetable equivalents of filaments. The yarns are twisted in the opposite direction to the fibres to form the strands, and the strands are twisted in the opposite direction to the yarns, to form the lay of the line. The main vegetable fibre ropes are coir, cotton, Italian hemp, Manila and sisal.

Figure of eight knot: a stopper knot that, because of its bulk, is often preferred to the thumb knot, being easier to undo although it does not bind so tightly.

To make this knot, lay the working end across the standing part, passing the former around behind the latter. The knot is completed by tucking the working end down through the bight (*figure 62*). It is not necessary to tighten the knot, as this will happen automatically when the knot is engaged; *see also* continuous figure of eight; double figure of eight; figure of eight loop; figure of eight in a double end, and sliding figures of eight.

figure 62, **above**

figure 63.1, **right**

Figure of eight in a double end: this variation of the figure of eight knot provides a stopper knot with a loop, and is a better knot to use than a bowline when tying a very slippery synthetic fibre.

Form the knot by making a large bight in the end of the rope, which is then used to tie the figure of eight (*see* page 80); *figure 63.1* shows the forming of the knot and *figure 63.2* the completed knot.

figure 63.2

Figure of eight loop: this is the same as the figure of eight tied in a double end, except that it is formed differently. It is of particular use when the loop cannot be dropped over a bollard, but is being tied through a ring or eye.

Tie a figure of eight some way back along the standing part from the working end, then pass this through the ring and back up through the lower

bight of the figure of eight. Finally, pass this around behind the standing part and bring it forward to weave over the front of the figure of eight, under its own bight (which forms the required loop) and out over the other side of the figure of eight (*figure 64*).

Figure of eight loop on the bight: used when the final loop can be dropped over a post or bollard.

Make the figure of eight loop by taking a large bight in the end of the rope and use this to form a figure of eight by taking it across and around behind one standing part. This is where this knot differs from the figure of eight tied in a double end, in that you then take the bight around only one of the standing parts (*figure 65.1*) before tucking it through the bight; therefore, it separates the standing parts (*figure 65.2*).

Filament: this is the smallest element of material that is used to form the individual fibres of synthetic rope. The main synthetic fibre ropes are nylon, polyester and polypropylene.

Fisherman's bend *see* **bucket hitch.**

figure 64

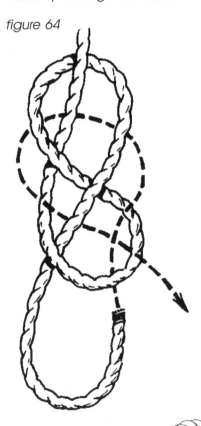

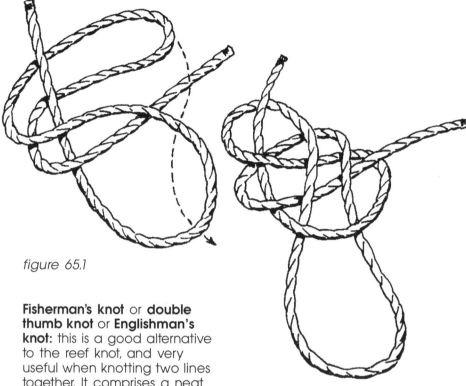

figure 65.1

figure 65.2

Fisherman's knot or **double thumb knot** or **Englishman's knot:** this is a good alternative to the reef knot, and very useful when knotting two lines together. It comprises a neat arrangement of two thumb knots, embedded tightly one against the other, with their short ends on opposite sides and lying virtually parallel to their nearest standing part.

figure 66

Begin by laying the two lines alongside each other, but facing in opposite directions. Then tie a thumb knot (*see* page 171) with one end around the standing part of

the other rope. Now reverse the lines and tie an identical thumb knot with the other end, enclosing its nearby standing part (*figure 66*). The two knots can now be pulled together to form the fisherman's knot.

Flat seizing: form an eye in the rope to the required size and then sew the rope together with twine, making three or four stitches at the same place but leaving about twice the thickness of the rope between the length of the stitches. Take round turns around the joined ropes until

the length of the stitches is covered. Now take the needle through the eye and make three cross-turns around the entire length of the round turns and pull the whole seizing tight. Use the remaining twine to sew round the cross-turns and through the rope before trimming off.

Flemish eye: a variation on the eye splice, made in the end of a rope.

Begin by carefully unlaying just one strand from the end of the rope, and form a bight in this single strand. At the point of the extremity of the required eye, relay the single strand into the vacant lay (*figure 67.1*) and work it

figure 67.1

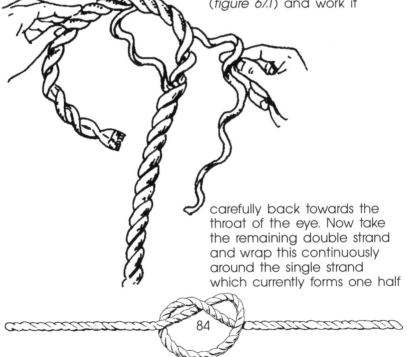

carefully back towards the throat of the eye. Now take the remaining double strand and wrap this continuously around the single strand which currently forms one half

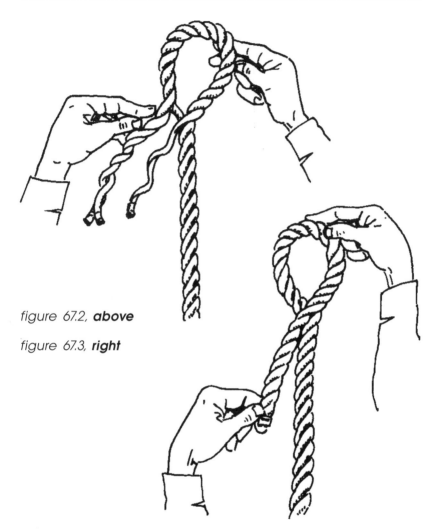

figure 67.2, **above**

figure 67.3, **right**

of the eye, using the single
strand to fill the vacant lay
until the double strand also
reaches the throat of the eye
(*figure 67.2*). The three strands
have now met again so that

you can lay back the single
strand into its original position
to form the working end
(*figure 67.3*), which is then
securely seized to the
standing part.

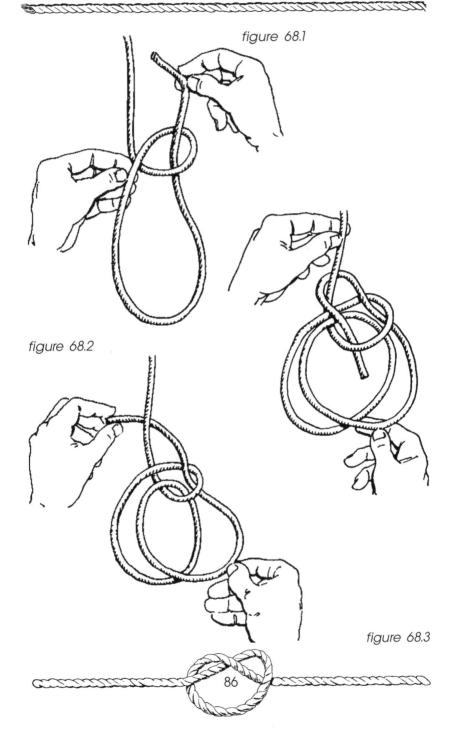

figure 68.1

figure 68.2

figure 68.3

Fool's knot *see* **Tom Fool's knot**.

Forming a knot: a knot may be first formed in the hands before being 'cast' (dropped) over the object to which it is being secured, a term applied mainly to hitches; alternatively, when it must be made around an object which has no available end, such as a continuous railing, the knot is 'turned' (formed) around the object.

Frapping turns: when applied to whipping, these are turns taken around the whipping parallel to, and in between, the ropes being seized together. The turns are best finished with a clove hitch (*see* page 40) and secured with a thumb knot (*see* page 171); *see also* flat seizing, racking seizing and round seizing.

French bowline or **Portuguese bowline:** this is a very good knot, as it produces two bights on a single end and it can be used as an alternative or quick bosun's chair, since a person can sit in one loop while the other loop goes around the back to provide support. We have illustrated the knot here on a much smaller scale for clarity.

The initial formation of the French bowline is exactly the same as for the ordinary bowline (*see* page 21) with the tail being laid across the standing part, which is lifted over to form the bight with the end automatically taken up and through (*figure 68.1*). Now take the end in a complete full turn and return it up through the loop (*figure 68.2*), around the standing part and back through the bight (*figure 68.3*). Obviously for a bosun's chair the bights will need to be considerably larger than and of differing sizes to those indicated here.

French sennit (four-stranded): begin by securing the four strands at the top. In our illustration we arranged two lengths of cord side by side, then formed a bight at the mid-point and seized the four lengths together at a point that allowed for a small eye if required.

Working first with the inside left strand, take this over the inside right strand, so that these two strands have swapped positions. Next take the outside right strand over the inside right (remember this was originally the inside left strand), and the outside left strand under the inside left strand but over the inside right

figure 69

French sennit (seven-stranded): the same principle applies as for the narrower four-stranded French sennit, of weaving under one, over one, from the outside to the centre.

Secure the seven strands at the top and divide with three to one side and four to the other. Starting with the even side, take the outside strand and weave it under one, over one, under one so that it now becomes the central strand. Next take the outside strand from the other side (originally with the odd number of strands) and work that under, over, under, to arrive at the centre. Repeat this process, alternating from side to side, until the required length of plait is achieved.

French whipping: a simple decorative covering based on half hitches, and ideal for covering rails or ends where a good grip is necessary.

Secure a line to the object being covered with a clove hitch, and working with one end form a continuous series of half hitches around the object (*figure 70*). When the required length is reached you can finish the end with a decorative knot, such as a Turk's head.

strand. These last two movements can now be repeated: outside right over inside right, outside left under inside left and over inside right, and so on until the required length is reached; *figure 69* shows both the tightened plait, and lower down the loose plait, for clarity.

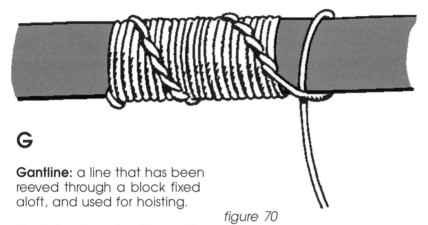

G

Gantline: a line that has been reeved through a block fixed aloft, and used for hoisting.

Gasket coil *see* **buntline coil**.

Granny knot: basically the poor, much-maligned granny is a mis-tied reef knot (*see* page 130), when one half has been tied forward and the other half backwards, so that the knot will not lie flat; in addition to which it will most often jam, making it difficult to untie.

figure 70

Grommet: a ring or strope made from a single strand of rope; the grommet is a practical piece of fancy work rather than a true knot, and perhaps is best employed to reinforce lacing holes.

figure 71.1

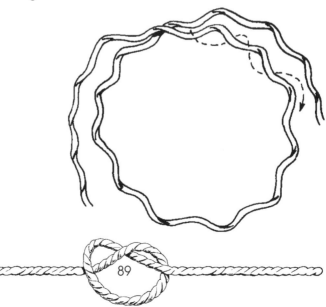

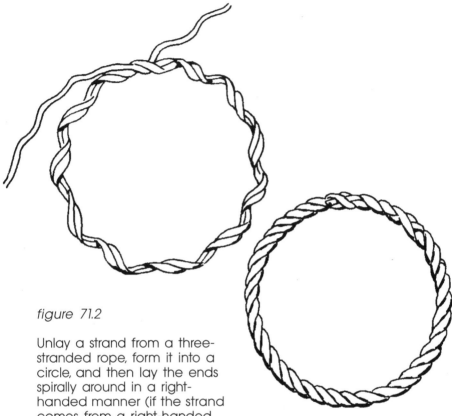

figure 71.2

Unlay a strand from a three-stranded rope, form it into a circle, and then lay the ends spirally around in a right-handed manner (if the strand comes from a right-handed rope) or in a left-handed manner if the strand comes from a left-handed rope (*figure 71.1*). Lay one end around and use the other end to fill in (*fig71.2*). When the circle is complete, tuck the ends against the lay (*figure 71.3*) to complete the grommet.

Ground line hitch: a tough knot, said to have been used

figure 71.3

by cavalrymen to tether their horses to a picket rope.

It is formed like a clove hitch (*see* page 40), but instead of the working end finally being passed under the turn, it goes across the turn and under the first turn from the standing part, which then holds the end in place.

figure 72

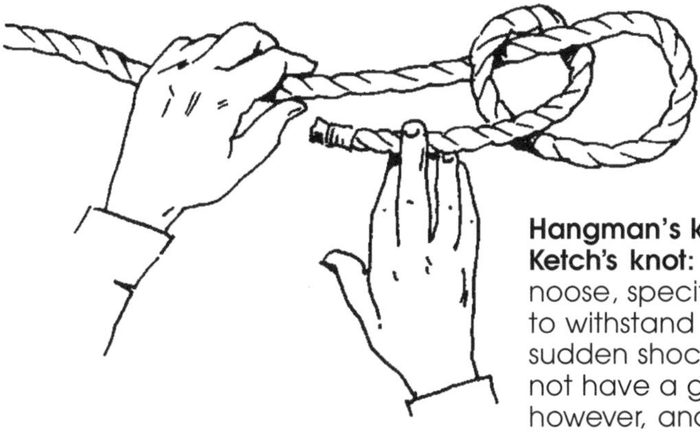

Hangman's knot or **Jack Ketch's knot:** a very strong noose, specifically designed to withstand a heavy and sudden shock loading. It does not have a good sliding ability however, and therefore needs to be adjusted to the required size when being formed.

H

Half blood knot *see* **three and a half turn clinch knot**.

Half hitch: not particularly useful in itself; however, the half hitch does form the basis of many other knots.

It is formed by making a bight, perhaps by looping a rope around a post or other object, bringing the working end around the standing part to take a partial turn (*figure 72*), and then pulling the two ends in opposite directions so that the half hitch tightens. Do remember though, that the half hitch will not hold on its own and needs to be finished off either by making the ends secure under tension, or with another knot.

Half hitch coil *see* **coiling**.

figure 73.1

Hard lay or **tight lay:** a rope is said to be hard laid when it has been tightly twisted.

Haul: to pull a rope through a block or knot, or to tug a line tight.

Hawser: a term that generally applies to all three-stranded right-handed ropes, but more properly defines a very large rope of over 38mm (1.5in) diameter; that is, big enough for towing or mooring but which is not a cable.

Hawser laid: a three-stranded right-handed rope (*figure 74*).

figure 74

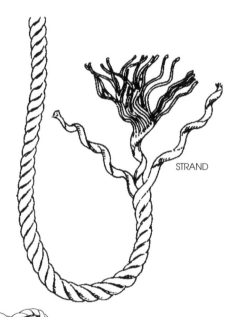

STRAND

figure 73.2

Form a bight in the rope and then a second bight, so that the rope goes back on itself to form a figure 'S'. Take seven turns around all three parts of the rope (*figure 73.1*) before passing the end through the remaining bight at the top. To secure it, pull the lower loop hard downwards, which locks the end against the turns (*figure 73.2*).

Heart or **core:** a loosely twisted strand or even yarns or filaments, which run the length of larger ropes of more than three strands, to form a central filler or heart. They can also be found in most braided lines; see **Admiralty eye splice.**

Heaving line: a heaving line is a 'messenger', a light throwing line usually of between 10 to 15mm (0.4 to 0.6in) diameter, and about 25m (82ft) long, subsequently used to haul a heavier rope ashore. The end of the heaving line must also be weighted in order to assist the throwing (see heaving line knot and monkey's fist). The thrower should keep his or her end of the line secure, and not attach it to the cable until after it has been successfully thrown; see also coiling a heaving line and throwing a heaving line.

figure 75

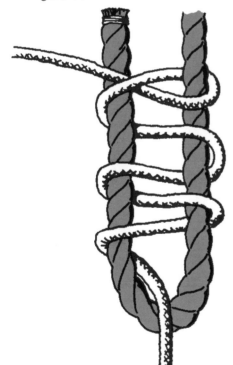

Heaving line bend: used to bend the heaving line to the warp; this is quite simply a bight formed in the end of the mooring warp, with the heaving line passed through it and racked back and forth across its two parts, finally being pulled tight and finished off with a half hitch (*figure 75*).

Heaving line knot: tied in the throwing end of the heaving line, to provide the necessary weight to enable the line to be thrown accurately, yet soft enough not to cause the recipient any damage.

First form two bights in the end of the rope to form an 'S', and take the end through the first bight before taking a turn around the two parts of the first bight (*figure 76.1*). Follow this with about five turns

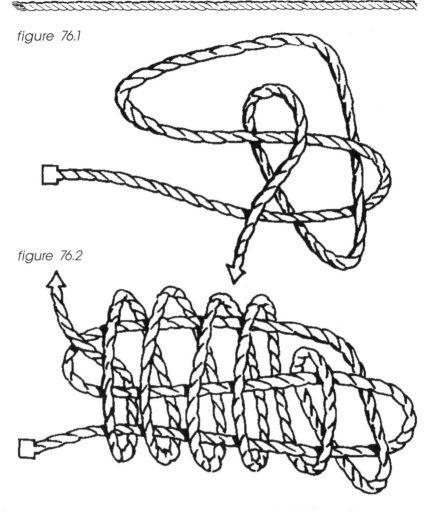

figure 76.1

figure 76.2

around all parts and finish by taking the end out through the eye of the second bight (*figure 76.2*). Pull tight on the standing part to complete the knot.

Hemp: an old type of natural vegetable fibre rope, and the strongest. Although it weathers badly this can be countered by tarring the rope. Italian tarred hemp is traditionally regarded as the best available. Large quantities of hemp also came from Russia until the mid-1800s, when it was replaced by

Manila hemp. This was itself replaced by man-made fibres after the Second World War. Some specialist shops are still able to provide small quantities of Manila hemp.

Highwayman's cutaway *see* **highwayman's hitch**.

Highwayman's hitch or **highwayman's cutaway:** as you might expect from its name, this is a slippery hitch, supposedly designed for the rapid release of a horse's tether by fleeing robbers.

Form a bight in the rope and pass it up behind the post. Now pull the standing part up in front of the post and between the bight at the back. This will form another bight, through which the working end is pulled (*figure 77.1*), to form a third bight (*figure 77.2*). Pressure applied to the standing part will not budge the hitch, but a swift downward tug on the end will release the rope from the post completely.

figure 77.1

figure 77.2

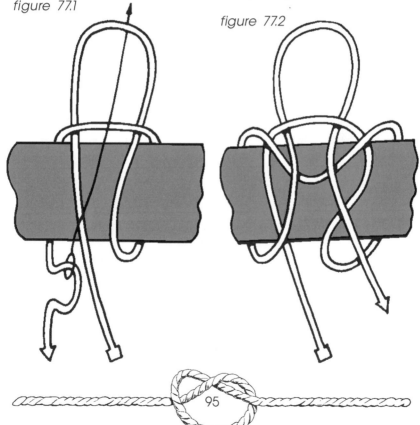

Hitches: a knot that secures a rope to an object, often as a temporary measure only, and thus one that can be undone or removed quite easily. One advantage of a hitch is that it can be made directly about an object, such as a post, without having to be formed first; *see also* backwall hitch, bucket hitch, clove hitch (cast), clove hitch (turned), cow hitch, cow hitch and toggle, draw hitch, half hitch, highwayman's hitch, killick hitch, lighterman's hitch, midshipman's hitch, rolling hitch, scaffold hitch, spar hitch, timber hitch and wagoner's hitch.

Horn: a small piece of timber, attached at right angles to the back of a stage (*see* page 160). It acts to prevent the stage hitch from slipping off the end of the stage. One leg of the horn is longer than the other, which provides a space between the ship's side and the stage, through which a person's legs will fit when sitting on the stage; *see also* stage and scaffold hitch.

Hunter's bend or **rigger's bend** or **zeppelin bend:** a recently-introduced bend, often employed in place of a sheet bend. It was designed specifically to join two lines made of smooth, synthetic materials. The bend is simply tied, and is based upon two interlocking thumb knots (*see* page 171).

Place the two lengths of rope side by side, and form a bight in both (*figure 78.1*), with no accidental crossover of ropes. Now tuck each working end through the bight from opposite sides (*figure 78.2*). The knot must now be worked tight by pulling on the standing parts. The rear view of the finished knot is shown in *figure 78.3*. You will note that the knot turns about itself as you carefully haul it tighter.

figure 78.1

figure 78.2

figure 78.3

I

Improved blood knot:
originally a fishing knot, this is used to join together two lines of unequal thickness, when the difference in thickness is too great for the basic blood knot (*see* page 19) to be efficient. The one drawback when using the improved blood knot is in the tightening; unless the turns are pulled up snugly the knot will lose strength. Generally it is the heavier line that will not tighten completely. For this reason the number of turns used is varied for each line, and here anglers must use their own experience and judgment.

The improved blood knot is tied in exactly the same manner as the basic blood

figure 79

knot, apart from the variation in the number of turns already mentioned, and the fact that a very light line must be doubled. The doubled light line with five turns and three turns in the heavier line shown in *figure 79* illustrate just such a situation. We suggest that next you first moisten the loose knot and then, with a cloth wrapped around each hand to avoid them being cut, you jerk the knot sharply to seat it. Here again you will profit from experience, and it should be borne in mind that if it is necessary for you to make a second tug to get the knot to seat properly, then this will weaken the knot. When the knot has been tightened, trim the working ends.

Improved clinch knot, improved, or **tucked, half blood knot:** although the basic three and a half turn

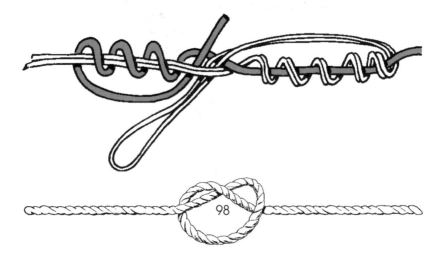

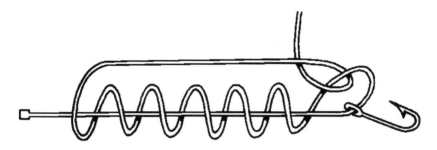

figure 80

clinch knot (*see* page 170) provides a breaking strength of some 80 per cent, the improved clinch knot, with its breaking strength of at least 95 per cent, is perhaps the most favoured way of tying a line to a hook, lure or swivel. The crucial difference of the improved knot is that five turns are taken around the standing part.

Insert the working end through the eye of the hook and allow yourself about 15 to 20cm (6 to 8in) to tie the knot. Using pliers to hold the hook in your right hand, take five turns around the standing part before passing the end through the loop which has been formed between the eye of the hook and the first turn, and back through the bight that you have just created between the working end and the turns around the standing part (*figure 80*). Now

moisten the knot and pull steadily on the standing part while holding the pliers with the hook in your other hand to tighten the knot. Very fine line may be doubled for the tying of the improved clinch knot.

Improved half blood knot *see* **improved clinch knot**.

Improved turle knot: this is not as strong as, for example, the improved clinch knot, but it was designed specifically to ensure that the pull on the hook remains straight, with the eye of the fly turned down.

Insert the working end of the line through the eye of the hook so that it passes from the top of the eye to the bottom. Pull through about 30cm (12in) of line and take a turn around the standing part, bringing the working end through the bight of the turn

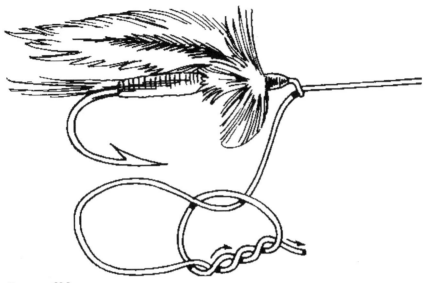

figure 81.1

figure 81.2

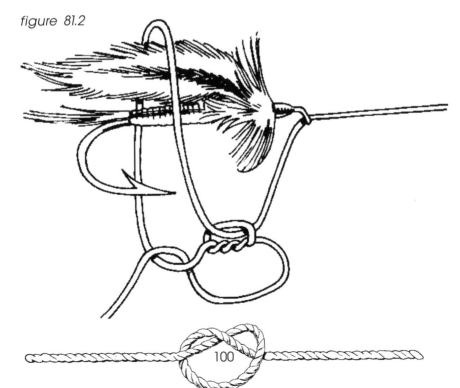

twice (*figure 81.1*). Here you have created a loose slip knot, which is tightened as follows: hold the working end in one hand and the big loop in the other. Pull both hands apart, and this will tighten the slip knot. Now pass the big loop over the fly (*figure 81.2*), and at the same time take the working end and pass it through the lower side of the loop. This provides a little extra strength in the knot. Pull the standing part slowly to tighten the knot, while ensuring that the line has cleared the hackles of the fly. You can now trim the end quite close, and the finished knot will enable you to exert a straight pull on the fly.

J

Jack Ketch's knot *see* **hangman's knot**.

Jury mat: this is based on the jury mast head knot (*see* page 103) with the four bights being arranged as in *figure 82.1*. The central bights are then drawn out over one, under one, over one to the right and under one, over one, under one to the left (*figure 82.2*). The next move is to cross the new central bights, the right-hand bight over the left, and then reeve the working end (shown bottom right in *figure 82.1*) through the centre of the mat

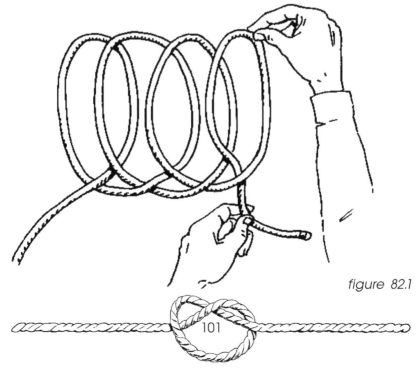

figure 82.1

figure 82.2

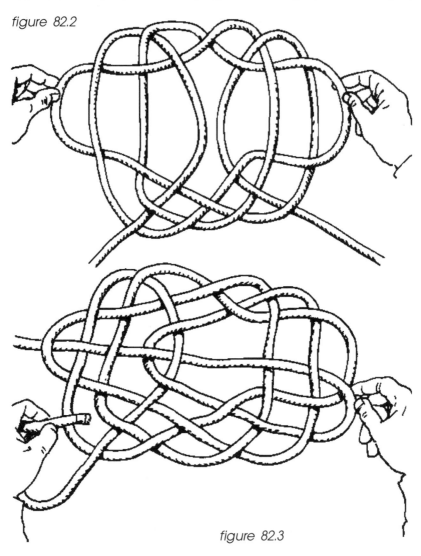

figure 82.3

from right to left continuously over one, under one (*figure 82.3*). Take the working end down to meet the standing part and use it to 'follow round' the original formation to fill in the skeleton twice to complete the mat (*figure 82.4*).

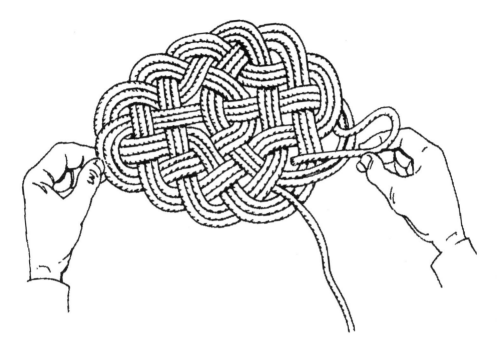

figure 82.4

Jury mast head knot: used as a temporary measure in an emergency rigging of a jury mast, and is placed at the mast head to form the band to which the stays and shrouds of the jury mast are secured. The greater the strain set up in the rigging, the tighter the knot will grip the mast. It is made in the centre of a rope with sufficient line to provide for the backstay(s).

Begin by laying down three bights (*figure 83.1*) which are then arranged one on top of another as in *figure 83.2*. Then rearrange these so that the left-hand part of the right-hand side (or lower) bight lies on top of the right-hand part of the left-hand side (or top) bight, with their overlapping in the centre on the middle bight. Now pass your hands (*figure 83.3*) under and over the outer bights to pick up the two overlapping bights in the centre. Pull these two bights out so that they weave over and under the outer loops. Once out, you can pull up the loop lying at the top to

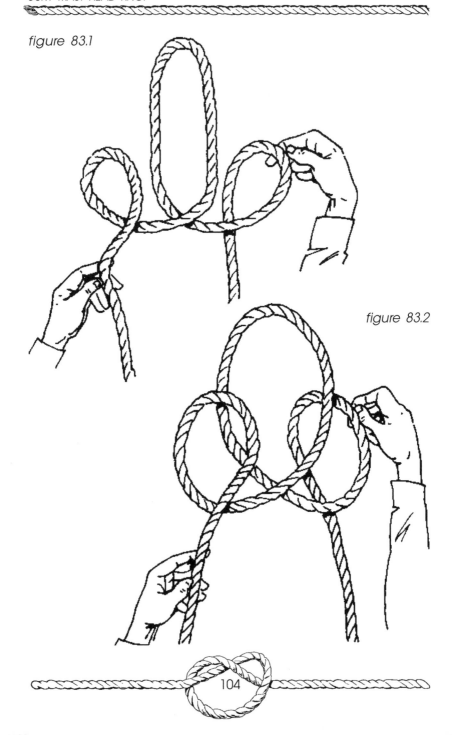

figure 83.1

figure 83.2

give a clover-leaf effect
(*figure 83.4*), with three loops
to which the shrouds and
forestay can be attached.
The mast sits in the centre of
the knot, and the two ends of
the rope are tied together
with a bowline (*see* page 21),
the long end forming the
back stay.

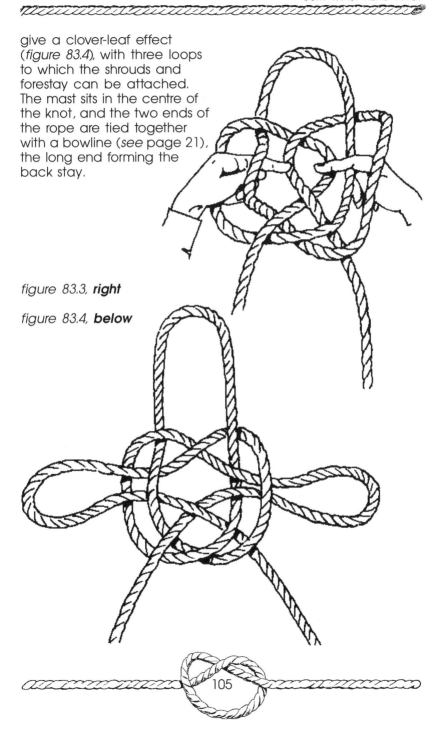

figure 83.3, **right**

figure 83.4, **below**

K

Karabiner *see* **carabiner**.

Kernmantel rope: specifically for climbers, it comprises a sheath and a core. It is a specialised rope designed to absorb shock by means of its elasticity.

Kevlar: a relatively expensive pale-gold coloured aromatic polyamide fibre made by Du Pont. It is used mainly for halyards and spinnaker guys, and has the highest strength to weight or diameter ratio of any fibre used in ropes. This is mainly because of the use of carbon fibres in its manufacture. Kevlar has virtually no stretch, and loses only five per cent of its strength when spliced.

Killick hitch: an ideal hitch to use for towing, or lifting poles or any other long objects, whether they are bulky or thin. It is composed of a timber hitch (*see* page 173) with a half hitch (*see* page 91) added at a distance from the original knot (*figure 84*).

Knot: strictly speaking, a knot is tied only in a single piece of rope; for example when being tied as a stopper in the end of a rope, or when the end of a line is passed through a bight in itself, or when the two ends of the same piece of cord are used to tie a parcel. However, the term has been extended generally to cover the joining together of two pieces of very small lines, though these are more properly classified as bends. For an explanation of

figure 84

the basic terms used to denote the various parts of a rope in which a knot is being formed, *see* bight, working end, and standing part.

Knot strength: the capacity of the knot to withstand a load without breaking the rope. It must be borne in mind that all knots weaken rope, with the exception of the Bimini twist (*see* page 14). This has a claimed knot strength of 100 per cent, that is, as strong as the line. Sharp turns within a knot lead to the loss of strength; therefore hitches, where large turns are often employed, are generally more efficient than knots. Examples are the clove hitch, which has a 75 per cent efficiency, and individual splices which are sometimes recognised as being up to 90 per cent efficient.

L

Lanyard: a line used to secure the rigging on sailing vessels. The term also applies to a small line attached to personal items of equipment, to prevent their loss.

Lark's head *see* **cow hitch.**

Lay: describes the direction in which the strands of the rope

were twisted in its manufacture, either right-handed or left-handed. It can also describe the nature of that twist; tight (hard), medium, or loose (soft).

Lead: the direction followed by the working end through the knot.

Lighterman's hitch: this is a hitch that needs to be under a constant strain, but it does present a quick way of making a temporary eye in the end of a rope, and is formed by following the early stages of a bowline.

figure 85.1

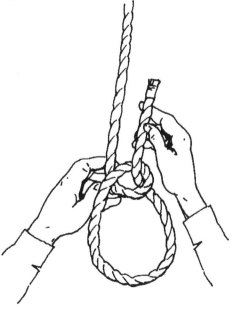

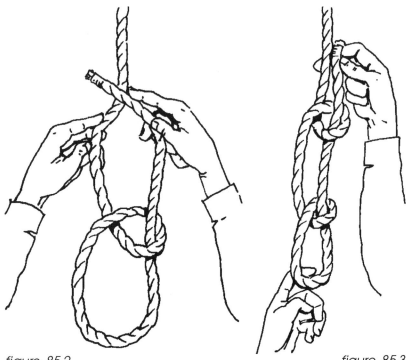

figure 85.2   figure 85.3

Form a bight in the end of the rope and thread the end up through it (*figure 85.1*). This stage can be reached in a quicker, more professional manner as described for the forming of a bowline (*see* page 21). Now take the end farther along the standing part (*figure 85.2*), and repeat the initial movement to arrive at the finished hitch (*figure 85.3*).

Line: a general term used for unspecified cordage.

Liverpool eye splice or **wire eye splice:** one of many similar splices, the Liverpool eye splice is a straightforward splice, tucked with the lay and devoid of locking turns. It is, therefore, not suitable for extra-heavy loads, such as for crane wires. In addition, the latter also have a tendency to twist, which would eventually lead to the unlaying of the splice. It is thus not as efficient as the Admiralty eye splice (*see* page 6).

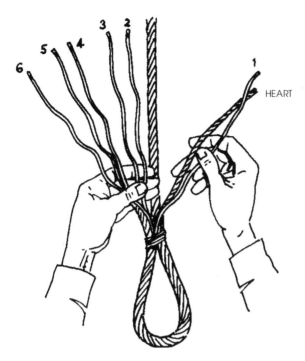

figure 86.1

Start by applying a whipping about 60cm (24in) from the end of the wire, and then unlay the wire up to that point. Take good care when doing this to ensure that the working strands are maintained in their correct order, 1 to 6, as this is the sequence for tucking.

For ease of working, we suggest that the heart or core (*see* page 93) is cut out at this stage , and that the ends of the strands are given a sharp twist with a pair of pliers so that they cannot catch when being tucked. If you are using a thimble, as shown in *figure 86.2*, put it in place now and hold it tight with a clamp while you apply seizings to both shoulders. A third seizing could be added to the crown for extra tightness. If the eye is being formed without a thimble, then the standing part must be seized to the end at the point where the whipping had earlier been applied (*figure 86.1*).

Drive a spike through the standing part of the wire from the left, dividing it with three strands to the right and three strands plus the heart (if you have not cut this out) to the left. Make the first tuck with the strand one (this will be the strand on the far right), through the separated strands. Carefully withdraw the spike, but only enough for the end strand to drop off, leaving only two strands remaining on the right. Through this space tuck strand 2, which will have become the strand on the far right. Repeat this last movement by withdrawing the spike a little farther, so that another strand slips off, and there is now only one strand to the right. Pass through the next working strand, 3. The spike must now be withdrawn completely and re-entered, to separate the fourth strand of the standing part, through which you tuck working strand 4 (*figure 86.2*). Follow this last movement for strand 5, although the last strand, 6, has to be tucked under the same strand of the standing part as the first strand, but in the opposite direction. This now completes the first series

figure 86.2

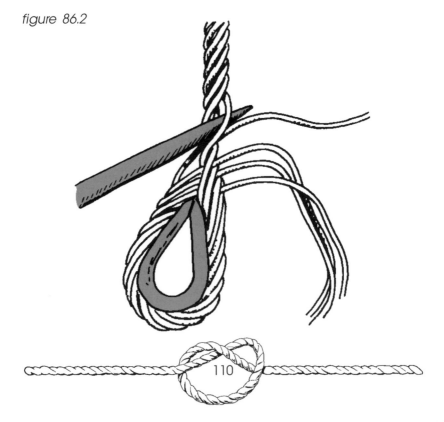

of tucks and the splice should be pulled tight, and the strands hammered more firmly into position.

For the next series of tucks it is easier to drive the spike in from the right. Having driven in the spike, twist it up towards the standing part. This action lifts the relevant strand and it will be easier for you to make the tuck. The tuck should be made towards the point of the spike. Tucking is done with the lay for the Liverpool eye splice.

figure 86.3

You can now either follow one strand around or work all six in sequence, but basically the working strand is wound spirally around the strand that it has been tucked beneath. We suggest an average of about five and a half tucks as being sufficient for small work. This will actually be three strands with six tucks and three strands with five tucks, which will mean that they will all emerge at the same point along the standing part.

To finish off the splice, hammer it tight with a mallet, working from the eye backwards down the splice, twisting the wire as you go. Trim off any ends and remove the seizing (*figure 86.3*).

Long splice: the great advantage of this splice, provided that it is correctly executed, is that it retains the diameter of the rope, thus allowing the rope to continue to run through existing blocks and eyes.

Begin by unlaying the strands of both ropes for a distance of about twelve turns, and then position the ends of the ropes opposite to each other and touching. Arrange the strands from the left-hand end to alternate with those of the right-hand end. Now unlay

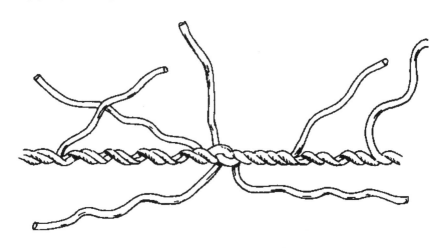

figure 87.1

one strand from each rope a further turn and replace it in the rope with its opposite number from the other rope. Continue doing this for a further five turns. (*Figure 87.1* shows the total extent of the unlaying for clarity, but you should fill the space left by the unlaid strand, after each turn, by its opposite number).

When complete, the finished result will look like a continuous piece of rope, with three pairs of strands along the rope. These must now be knotted together by means of a thumb knot (*see* page 171) (*figure 87.2*, centre). Cut the ends to equal lengths (*figure 87.2*, left) and halve them by reducing the number of yarns, before tucking them against the lay (*figure 87.2*, right).

figure 87.2

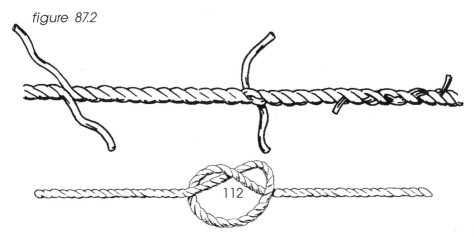

Loop: a bend in the rope where its standing parts come together or cross; also called a **bight** or an **eye**.

Loose lay *see* **soft lay**.

Lorry driver's hitch *see* **wagoner's hitch**.

M

Magner's hitch *see* **rolling hitch**.

Magnus hitch *see* **rolling hitch**.

Make fast: to belay (*see* page 8) or to secure a rope by means of a hitch.

Man harness *see* **chair knot**.

Manila: a natural fibre which is still available, and used on the rigging of a few traditional sailing vessels. Originating from the Far East, it became the most important cordage prior to the Second World War, especially in the larger sizes. It is, however, 20 per cent weaker than hemp.

Manrope: a rope hand rail, which is led through stanchions along a gangway.

Manrope knot: a permanent stopper knot, with the principal purpose of ensuring

figure 88.1

that the rope does not unreeve through an eye or block; as such, it performs the function of ending a manrope. The knot is made as described in this simple verse:

First a wall
Then a crown
Now tuck up
Then tuck down.

Begin by unlaying the rope and loosely form a wall knot (*see* page 187) with the three strands emerging upwards (*figure 88.1*). Now make a crown knot (*see* page 57), also kept loose. The tails are now hanging downwards. Then take the ends and follow around the wall knot; you will find that the tails will have laid neatly alongside the strands of the wall, and that after completing the doubled wall knot they lie neatly with the strands of the original crown. These are also followed around to complete the manrope knot with the tails taken back down through the centre of the knot to protrude at the bottom (*figure 88.2*), where they can be cut close to the knot.

figure 88.2

Marline or spunyarn: an impregnated cordage available throughout a large range of sizes and grades of quality. Mainly used as a form of protection to bind splices, it can also be used as a whipping on very large ropes.

Marlow eye splice: this is an eight-plait eye splice, and suitable for 9 or 10mm (0.4in) diameter ropes on dinghy sheets, as it has no great strength.

First tie a figure of eight loop (*see* page 82), about 2m (6ft 6in) from the end of the rope. The effect of this will be to prevent the outer plait from being disturbed beyond the area where you are making the splice.

Slide the outer plait back to reveal the inner core, from which you need to cut off 70cm (27.5in). Then slide the outer plait back to its full extent to leave a hollow sheath. Unlay 100mm (4in) of the outer plait and taper it in 25mm (1in) steps so that it can be threaded through the eye of the splicing tool. Work the splicing tool, eye first, into the hollow sheath about 15mm (0.6in) from the end of the inner core. It should re-emerge through the sheath wall about 300mm (12in)

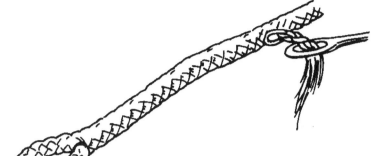

figure 89

away. Now thread the tapered plait yarns through the eye of the splicing tool and pull the tool back through the sheath. The plait will follow, filling the 300mm (12in) of hollow sheath (*figure 89*). The splice is now complete, and leaves you with an eye of about 100mm (4in) circumference at the end. The surplus yarn should be trimmed off once you have ensured that the splice is smoothed out, and then the figure of eight loop can be untied.

Mast head knot *see* **jury mast head knot.**

Matthew Walker (double): similar to the single version of the knot (*see* page 116),

except that the first strand is taken around the standing part, under the other two strands and brought up through its own bight (*figure 90.1*). The second strand is taken around the standing part, under the third strand,

figure 90.1

up through the bight of the first strand, and on through its own bight (*figure 90.2*). The third and last strand is brought around the standing part, up through both bights in turn and on up through its own bight and the knot worked tight to finish.

figure 90.2

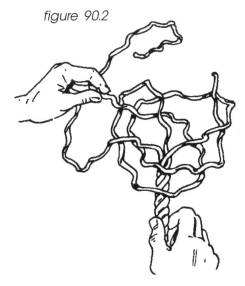

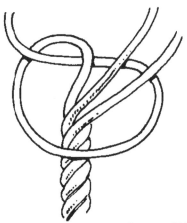

figure 91.1

91.1). Take the second strand around and pass it up through the first bight and retain a second bight. Repeat with the third strand following

figure 91.2

Matthew Walker (single): an attractive stopper knot, usually made on laid rope at any position throughout its length. They may also be made at the end of a rope, when the tails are whipped.

Form this knot by passing each strand around the rope in the direction of the lay under the other two strands, while retaining a bight (*figure*

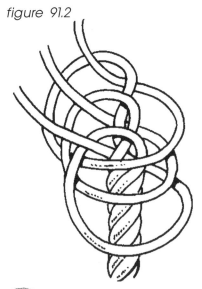

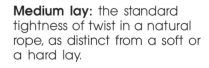

around and up through the first bight, then on and up through the second bight (*figure 91.2*). Then you can carefully work tight and finish off the knot (*figure 91.3*).

figure 91.3, **below**

figure 92, **below right**

Medium lay: the standard tightness of twist in a natural rope, as distinct from a soft or a hard lay.

Messenger, *see* **heaving line**.

Midshipman's hitch: a simple variation on the backwall hitch (*see* page 8), but more secure.

Take the rope over the hook and take a full turn around the entire hook before finishing with a half hitch (*figure 92*). The hitch will hold fast, provided a constant pressure is applied to the standing end.

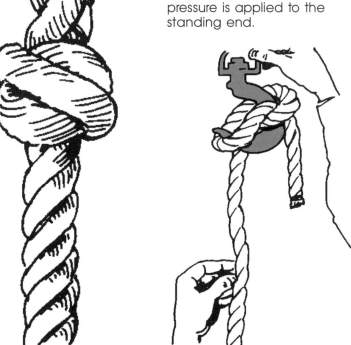

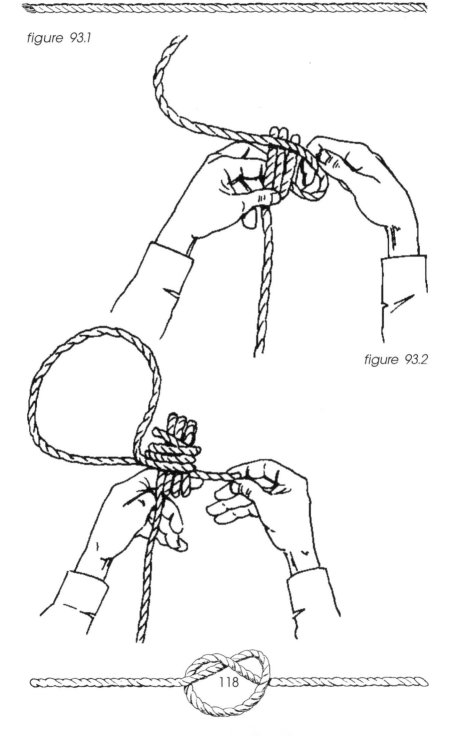

figure 93.1

figure 93.2

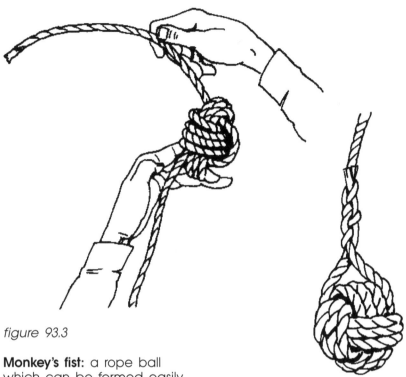

figure 93.3

Monkey's fist: a rope ball which can be formed easily, often used at the end of a heaving line to provide it with carrying weight. It is sometimes formed with a metal or wooden ball (as of course the latter will float) inserted into the weave, to provide additional carrying weight.

Measure off about 1.5m (5ft) of line and begin to work from this point back towards the tail end of the rope, first by forming three turns (*figure 93.1*). Follow these by a further

figure 93.4

three turns, passed around the original three but at right angles to them (*figure 93.2*). A third and final set of three turns is made around the second group but inside the initial group (*figure 93.3*). It is at this point that any ball to be used should be inserted into the centre of the fist, before it is worked tight to take all of the slack out. Cut off and work the working end into the standing part (*figure 93.4*).

Monofilament line: a single strand of nylon, available in a wide range of breaking strengths. It is the most popular type of line in use today with anglers. After a period of time, however, the monofilament will loose some of its properties, resulting in a reduction of its breaking strength, and thus the angler needs to check his or her line and replace it if necessary.

N

Natural rope: all the kinds of cordage made from natural vegetable fibre, including coir, hemp, jute, Manila, raffia and sisal.

Needle and palm whipping or **sewn whipping:** the palm refers to a leather guard worn around the hand and which is used to push the needle through the rope. Sewn whipping by needle and palm is both permanent (it will not slip off the end) and tidy.

Start by anchoring the end of the twine with a couple of stitches through the rope. Pass turns around the rope, working towards the working end, but make sure that they are both tight and snug to each other. When you have made sufficient turns (we suggest that together, they should be equal to the diameter of the rope) pass the needle through a strand at the top of the rope (*figure 94.1*) and work the twine back over the turns so that it lies in a natural groove between two strands of the rope. Stitch though the next strand at the bottom of the whipping, and take the twine to the top again via another groove, to repeat the operation up and down the whipping until all of the spiral

figure 94.1

figure 94.2

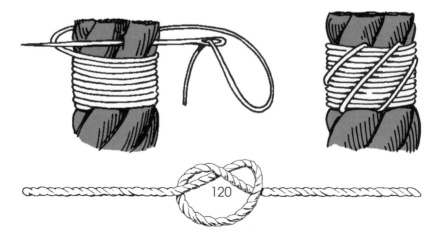

turns are doubled. Secure the end of the twine by taking extra stitches through the rope, and the whipping is complete (*figure 94.2*).

Sail or whipping twine can be used, but for sheathed ropes both core and sheath must be stitched together.

Netting: simple to make, netting is used on board a ship to fill the space between the guardrail and the deck in addition to being used to provide additional stowage space, for example above a berth.

You will need a shuttle to carry the twine for net making, and these are easy to obtain from chandlers and craft shops.

For the guardrail net, first make a row of clove hitches (*see* page 40) along the life line above each square of mesh; a spacer of suitable size should be used to ensure even spacing. The bottom of the net is led through a hole in the toe rail, but we have adapted our illustration (*figure 95.1*) for clarity, using a bar instead. Form a sheet bend (*see* page 149) (*figure 95.2*) on the bight of each loop a line at a time, until the space is covered (*figure 95.1*).

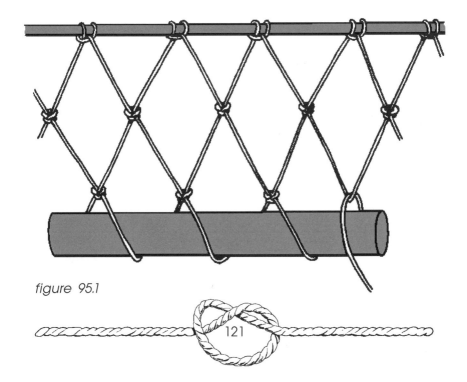

figure 95.1

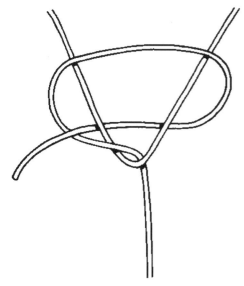

figure 95.2

Net line knot: a fisherman's knot which is basically a ground line hitch (*see* page 90) with an extra turn, which provides extra security against lengthwise pulls.

Make a round turn by taking the end from right to left across the front of the spar, bring the turn across the front to trap the standing part to the spar, and then take a second turn bringing the end over the two turns just made from bottom right to top left, tucking it under the standing part where it first turns over the top of the spar.

Nip: refers to the frictional pressure within a knot that gives it its binding and prevents it from slipping; the point in a knot where the parts grip each other.

Noose: a loop made secure around its own standing part, with a slip knot which will pull tight. This is an ideal way with which to start tying parcels.

Nylon *see* **polyamide**.

O

Ocean mat or **ocean plait:** even a simple ocean mat, such as the one we have illustrated and described below, requires a great deal of cordage to complete the plait.

Begin by forming two bights in the centre of the rope (*figure 96.1*) and twist both bights anticlockwise before crossing the crowns of the bights, left-hand sided bight over right-hand sided bight (*figure 96.2*). Now you can take the ends diagonally down from top to bottom through the centre of the bight. The top right end is first reeved under one, over two, under one, then the other end is reeved over one, under one, over one, under one, over one (*figure 96.3*). All

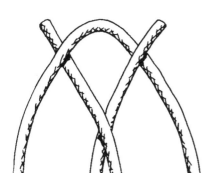

that remains to be done now is to follow the pattern around one end at a time, working each from bottom to top then from top to bottom. After three circuits the whole can be worked tight, the ends cut off and hidden under the mat.

Ocean plait *see* **ocean mat**.

figure 96.3

figure 96.1, **above**

figure 96.2, **below**

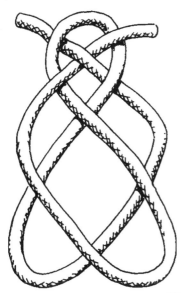

One-way sheet bend: this has the advantage over the basic sheet bend (*see* page 149) in that one end does not protrude at a right angle, which could lead to the knot becoming jammed.

Form a bight in the larger of the two ropes, and pass the other line up into this bight, before taking a turn around the neck of the bight. At this point when forming the basic sheet bend, the end is then tucked under itself to complete the knot; however, to form this variation the working end is taken under itself,followed by a turn around its own standing part, before being woven back through its own bight.

Overhand knot *see* **thumb knot**.

Overhand knot plait *see* **thumb knot plait**.

Overhand loop: a bight formed by holding the standing part of the rope in your left hand and, with the working end in your right hand, turning it to cross over the standing end, forming a full 360 degree turn. An underhand loop would be similarly formed, but by crossing the working end under the standing part.

P

Parcelling *see* **serving**.

Parts, relating to a **Turk's head:** this describes the number of strands seen if you could take a cross section through the knot prior to any follow round. It should be noted that the number of parts governs the length of the knot (*see* Turk's head page 176).

Perfection loop: a popular old knot for anglers who, with practice, are able to tie it quickly.

Holding the line in your right hand, about 150mm (6in) from the end and with your left hand a further 150mm (6in) distant, form a bight in the line by turning your right hand under your left, and secure the bight by sliding it along under your left thumb. Now take the working end in your right hand and make a loose second bight over your left thumb and around the first bight. Pass the working end under the first bight between the thumb and forefinger of your left hand, where you secure it (*figure 97.1*). Now pinch the second bight and push it through the first bight (*figure 97.2*). To tighten the knot (*figure 97.3*),

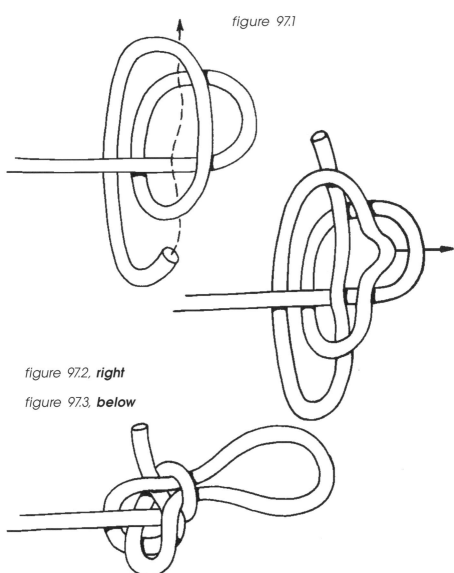

figure 97.1

figure 97.2, **right**

figure 97.3, **below**

pull on the standing part and the second bight (that is, the large loop on the right).

Although the knot ties easily in nylon, it will jam if tied in natural rope.

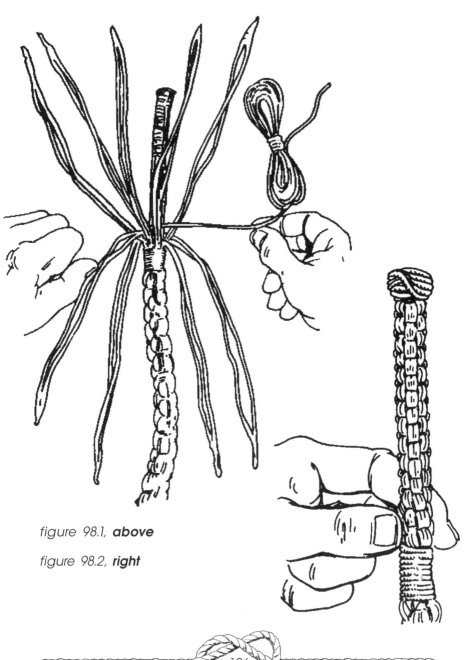

figure 98.1, **above**

figure 98.2, **right**

Pilot ladder *see* **rope ladder**.

Plaited rope or **braided rope:** a rope in which the strands are woven, as distinct from a laid rope. A plaited rope does not have any inherent twist or lay; it may or may not have a heart, and it may or may not be enclosed within a woven outer sheath.

For **plaits**, *see* chain plait, crown plait (spiral), crown plait (straight), diamond plait, double chain plait, eight plait, ocean mat, square plait, thumb knot plait (four-stranded), thumb knot plait (eight-stranded), twist plait, wall and crown plait, wall plait.

Pointing: provides a stiff tapered end to a rope, which thus enables it to be reeved speedily through a block.

Apply a whipping about 150mm (6in) from the end and unlay the perimeter strands. Keeping these 'working' strands out of the way, taper the remainder of strands and bind them. Tie a warping strand at the very top of the tapered strands and take a turn with it, interweaving the working strands (*figure 98.1*, in which we have paired the working strands). Now alter the positions of the working strands – all down strands up and all up strands down – then take a second turn with the warp. This procedure is repeated, dropping the odd strand as the taper narrows, until the point is reached. At this juncture the ends are secured with a whipping or a half hitch around the warp.

Alternative hitching patterns can be applied instead of the one up, one down just described, and the whole can be finished off with a Turk's head (*figure 98.2; see* page 176).

Polyamide: widely known as nylon; this is the strongest of the man-made synthetic fibres, with the exception of Kevlar and those which have been reinforced. It possesses excellent 'give', and as such is ideal for mooring and for anchor warps where shock loads are readily absorbed. Contrariwise it is unsuitable for sheets and halyards.

The rope will become hard in excessive sunlight, and cannot resist acid attack, although it stands up to alkalis; *see also* microfilament, polyester, polyethylene and polypropylene.

Polyester: marketed under the trade names of Dacron and

Terylene. Polyester is another man-made fibre, which follows after Kevlar and nylon in strength. It has a low stretch factor, is easy to handle and is thus quite suitable for all activities aboard a boat. It comes in both plaited and braided forms, and is also available pre-stretched. This further reduces its elasticity, helping to maintain a constant length. Polyester is resistant to acid attack.

Polyethylene: a cheap synthetic fibre, is difficult to knot because of its excessive stretching. It also loses its shape and becomes very slippery; in addition to these problems it has a tendency to retain kinks for a long time.

Polypropylene: a soft, malleable and cheap synthetic fibre rope, somewhat weaker than either polyester or nylon and with a poor resistance to abrasion. It can be knotted and spliced quite easily. Being buoyant it also makes a good heaving line. Polypropylene is resistant to attack by most acids and alkalis.

Portuguese bowline *see* **French bowline**.

Portuguese sennit (flat): the Portuguese sennits may be made with any number of strands, but only use two working strands, although these can be doubled, one on each side of the central strand(s) or heart. This central non-working heart can be any number of strands, although the shape of the sennit becomes difficult to maintain if you exceed three. Our illustrations show three strands in the heart and two single working strands.

Start working with the left-hand strand, and pass this under the heart(s) and over the right-hand strand. A bight must be retained on the left. Now take the right-hand strand across over the heart and down through the bight on the left. Now you can draw tight both ends, to complete the first knot.

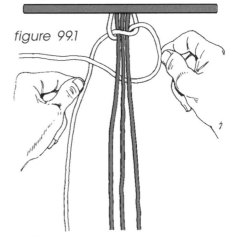

figure 99.1

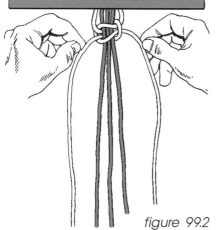

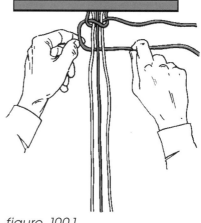

figure 99.2   figure 100.1

Take the right-hand strand and pass this under the heart and over the left-hand strand (*figure 99.1*). Now take the left-hand strand over the heart and through the bight on the right, drawing it tight to complete the second knot (*figure 99.2*). Repeat these two knots in sequence, continuing until you reach the length that you want.

Portuguese sennit (spiral): very similar to the flat Portuguese sennit (*see* page 128), being made by following the same method identically up to the completion of the first knot, when the left-hand strand is passed under the heart (*figure 100.1*) and over the right-hand strand, while the right-hand strand is crossed over the heart and through

the bight on the left. Draw tight the working strands to complete the second knot (*figure 100.2*). The knotting can be repeated, always using the left-hand strand first so that you will find that the spiral will develop automatically.

figure 100.2

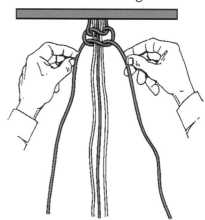

R

Racking seizing: is used whenever the strain on the two ropes being seized together is applied from opposite directions, or in place of a splice in braided rope where splicing is not always easy.

Begin by passing the seizing material around both ropes and then laying the turns in figure-of-eight fashion, taking the seizing between the two ropes. When enough turns have been made, usually ten or so, they are worked tight by means of a marline spike. The seizing can now be finished in the normal fashion. First form a half hitch (*see* page 91) around both rope parts, then apply a second layer of turns, known as riding turns, over the first layer, but not as tightly. Always take two less riding turns than the number of figure-of-eight turns, and this will prevent them from falling off at the ends. Bring the last riding turn up through to the front by passing it between the two parts of the rope, up through the original eye, before taking two or three frapping turns (*see* page 87) between the parts of the rope being seized. Finish by taking two or

three half hitches around the frapping turns, followed by a thumb knot, which should be worked tight.

If you are applying a racking seizing to wire rope, both parts of the wire should be covered with rigging tape in order to provide bite, and thus prevent the turns from slipping.

Reef bow: perhaps the most commonly used of all knots, and the one that all children start with, for the tying of shoe laces. The knot ties two ends together, and for slippery line the ends can be pulled through to form a reef knot (*see* page 130).

Begin by forming a thumb knot (*see* page 171), then make a bight in the end of each working end (*figure 101.1*) and form a second thumb knot. Pull the bights through but not the ends (*figure 101.2*).

Reef knot: a simple and quick way to join two ropes of similar size (*figure 102*).

figure 102

figure 101.1, **above**

figure 101.2, **below**

It is best traditionally described:

Left over right – twist through
Right over left – twist through
Haul tight.

NB: in America, this knot is known as the square knot.

Reeve: the act of passing the end of a rope through any aperture.

Riding turns: a second layer of turns, formed evenly and snugly though not so tightly that they force themselves into the first layer.

Rigger's bend *see* **hunter's bend**.

Rolling hitch or **Magner's hitch** or **Magnus hitch:** related to the clove hitch (*see* page 40) but more secure, being designed to take a lengthwise pull. It is often used to secure a smaller line to a thicker rope, and when so employed it should be tied against the lay of the rope that it is tied around.

Take a round turn around the spar, and follow this with a turn between the round turn and the standing part (*figure 103.1*) before finishing in the same way as you would normally finish a clove hitch (*figure 103.2*).

figure 103.2

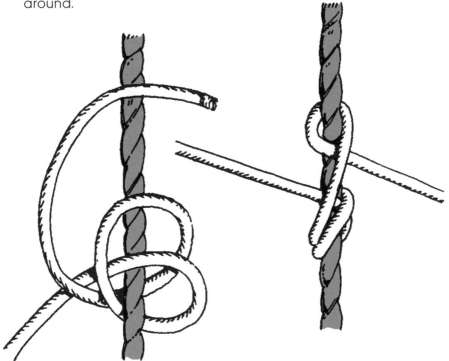

figure 103.1

Rope: the word used to describe any cordage over 10mm (0.4in) diameter.

A rope is comprised of three strands twisted together, usually in a right-handed spiral, although left-handed lay ropes are available. Each strand is composed of yarns which themselves have been twisted together, but in the opposite direction to the lay of the rope. Each yarn is composed of fibres, these being twisted together in the opposite direction to the lay of the yarns in the strand – that is, in the same direction as the lay of the rope. The effect of the alternating of the lay ensures that the rope binds tightly within itself and that it is less apt to become undone; *see also* fibres, hard laid, hemp, Kevlar, Manila, medium laid, natural rope, plaited rope, polyamide (nylon), polyester, polyethylene, polypropylene, shroud laid, 'S' laid, soft laid, staple, strands, synthetic rope, yarns and 'Z' laid.

Rope husbandry: although synthetic ropes can be stowed when wet, natural fibre rope needs to be dried out fully. All ropes need to be kept clean and free from grit, dirt and oil. Dirty rope should be washed thoroughly in clean fresh water; do not use detergents on natural fibres. Keep all ropes well clear of boilers, heating pipes and

flames. Remove kinks by coiling them and do not allow chafing. Any chafed or damaged ropes should be repaired or replaced immediately you notice them, as weak ropes can be dangerous.

Rope ladder knot or **pilot ladder:** the knot actually forms the rung of the rope ladder, which makes an ideal short climbing aid over the side of a boat for swimmers. It can be made on the bight of a rope with an eye, as illustrated in *figure 104*, or with twin tails at the top, which can be used to make it fast. We suggest using any strong thickish rope, of up to 15mm (0.6in) diameter.

Make a bight in the centre of the rope, and apply a strong seizing. Form two bights in the right-hand rope to form an S, then take the left-hand side rope into the first bight of the S, front to back. Then take a minimum of ten round turns, emerging from the back through the lower bight of the 'S'. You need to make the rung wide enough to accept your foot, but not too wide or it will sag. Now repeat the operation by making an S again with the right-hand (originally left-hand) rope, and turning the left-hand

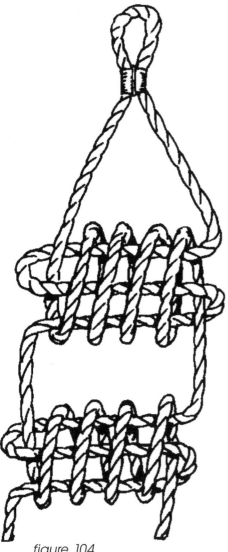

figure 104

continue for as many rungs as you require, or as the length of the rope permits. The formation of the rope ladder has been shown loose, and with just a few turns to form the rung, in *figure 104*. The rope should be hauled tight after each rung is completed.

Rope strength: vegetable fibre ropes are not as strong as their more recent cousins, the man-made fibre ropes. Furthermore, they are only half as strong when they are wet as when they are dry, and with the added disadvantage that they have a low strength to weight ratio. The thicker the natural fibre rope, the stronger it is. On the other hand, man made fibre ropes are light and strong; they do not loose strength when wet because they do not absorb water, so their breaking strength remains the same whether they are wet or dry. Synthetic rope does, however, deteriorate quickly at high temperatures; for example nylon melts at 250 degrees C.

Rose knot (four-stranded): a decorative stopper knot based on three other knots, the wall knot (*see* page 187), the crown knot (*see* page 57) and the diamond knot (*see* page 63).

rope around it as before. The rungs should be about 30cm (12in) apart, and you can

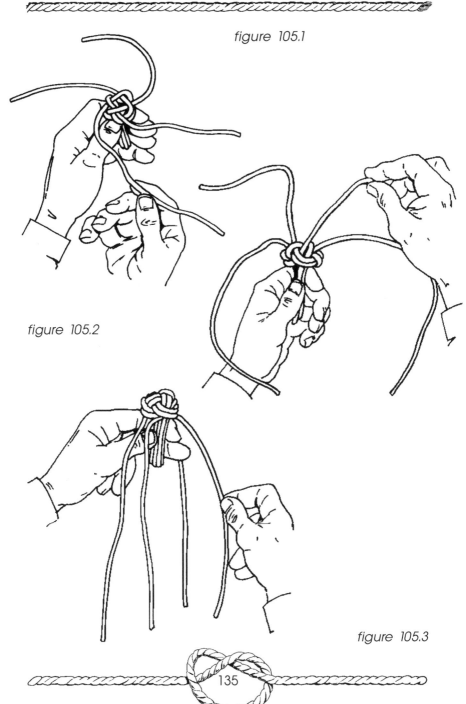

figure 105.1

figure 105.2

figure 105.3

Begin with a wall and crown (*see* page 185) (*figure 105.1*). Then completely follow around the wall but only partly follow around the crown (*figure 105.2*), and pass the strands down through the centre of the knot to emerge separately and hanging down (*figure 105.3*). Form another wall (*figure 105.4*), then a diamond knot which is followed around (*figure 105.5*) before you take all the ends back up through the centre and cut them short.

Round seizing: make an eye in the seizing material and then make sure that you are working against the lay.

Begin by passing the seizing around both parts of the rope, coming up through the eye, and then continue by making a further ten or so turns around both parts of the rope. It is important that this is done as tightly as possible; the aid of a mallet or marline spike is helpful in levering the seizing material tight after every third or so turn.

On completing the turns, form a half hitch around both rope parts, which will also help to hold the turns tight. Now add a second layer of turns. Known as riding turns, these

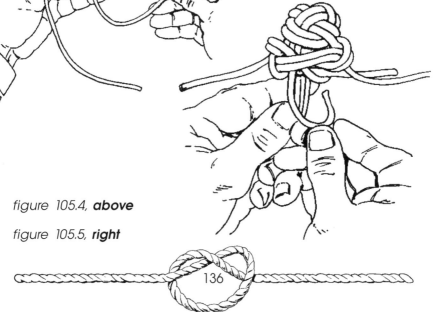

figure 105.4, **above**

figure 105.5, **right**

should be applied only hand tight so that they do not cut down into the lower layer, and thus they will leave a neater finish. Apply two fewer riding turns than for the first layer, so that they do not slip off the ends. Take the last riding turn up through the two parts of the rope, through the eye to the front, and take two or three frapping turns (*see* page 87) around the seizing, pulling these tight. To finish this knot, take two half hitches around both parts of the frapping turns.

Round sennit (four-stranded): the easiest to make of the round sennits, this makes an ideal lanyard or pull cord. Any number of strands can be used, four being the minimum.

Begin by seizing all four strands together at the top, then cross opposite pairs as follows. Starting with the strand to the right, pass this between its neighbours and behind the strand on the left. Now take that strand to the right, between its original neighbours. Take the top strand through its neighbours and to the right of the bottom strand, bringing that strand through its original neighbours to emerge at the front. For the next series of passes, again

figure 106

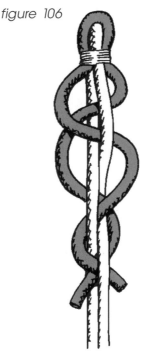

begin with the strand on the right, pass it through its neighbours, but in front of the strand on the left, taking that strand between its original neighbours to emerge on the right. Take the front strand, pass it through its neighbours to the left of the bottom strand, pulling that strand back to the top. All four strands are now back on the sides they started from, and the plait can be repeated (*figure 106*). The sennit can be finished with a decorative knot when you reach the required length.

Round turn: start with a turn (*see* page 181) of 360 degrees around the object, then take the end around a second time. This is then a round turn. It is worth remembering that the number of round turns taken is always one less than the number of sections of rope that you can see. Our illustration shows a round turn on the left and three round turns on the right of the rail (*figure 107*).

Round turn and two half hitches: the most commonly used hitch, used to secure a line to a post.

Make a round turn (*see* page 138) and secure it with two half hitches (*see* page 91), which should be worked

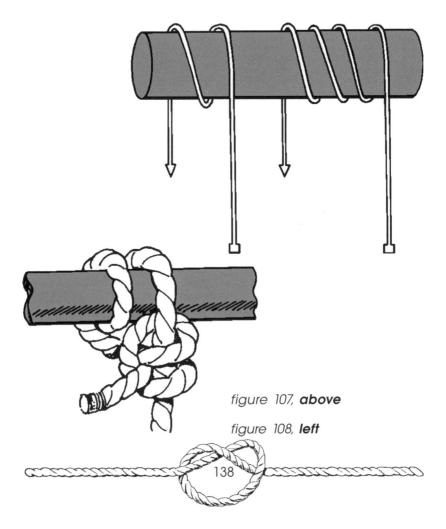

figure 107, **above**

figure 108, **left**

snugly against each other (*figure 108*).

Running bowline: a running knot that is formed by tying a bowline (*see page 21*) around a bight formed in, and not the standing part of, the rope (*figure 109*). The running

bowline forms an excellent secure noose.

Russian sennit (six-stranded): formed with the two outside strands used to act as borders, while all of the plaiting is done with the central strands, of which any number can be used.

Secure all of the strands at the top; if they are regularly spaced it will make the working easier, and the sennit can be hauled tight later.

Begin with the second strand from the left which becomes the first working strand, and take it around under the left-hand (border) strand, and back under the third strand from the left and lay it away to the left (*figure 110.1*).

Now take the next left strand, around under its right-hand neighbour, and lay it away to the left. (If we were making an eight-stranded Russian sennit, this movement would be repeated twice more, with each strand being laid away to the left.)

Now take the second strand from the right (the last working strand) under the outside right (border) strand and hold it there while you return all of the previously-worked central

figure 109

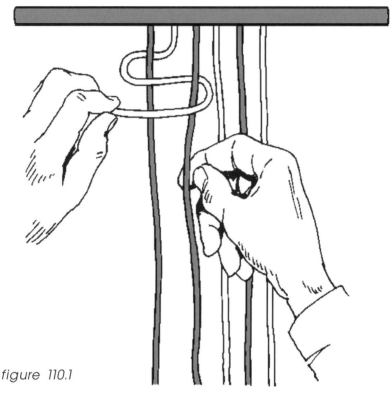

figure 110.1

strands to the vertical position. Now turn the strand you are holding to the right around the right-hand side border strand and then weave it from right to left under one but over all of the remaining strands on the left, and lay the strand away to the left. Take the next strand in from the right and reeve that under the strand to its left and over all of the remaining strands, laying it away to the left (*figure 110.2*). Repeat this last movement for all of the remaining strands except the far left (border) strand. Hold the last-worked strand to the left while you return all of the other strands to the vertical position (*figure 110.3*). This now completes the first 'over and back' working and you can repeat the whole operation until you reach the required length.

To finish, hitch the secured ends of all the strands

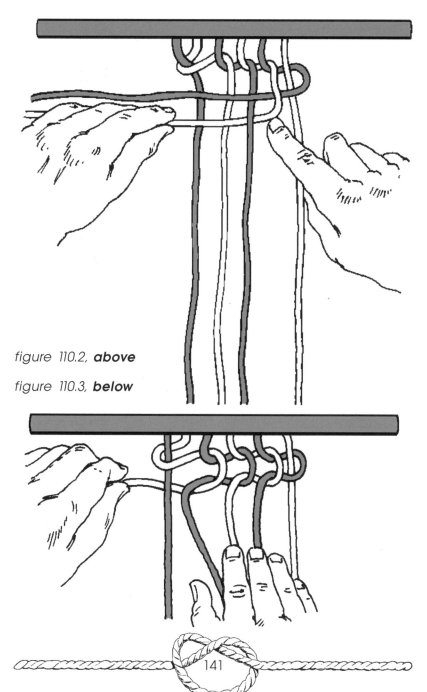

figure 110.2, **above**

figure 110.3, **below**

together; haul tight the working strands and hitch them together with the border strands at the other end.

S

Safe working load: the estimated load that a rope can bear without breaking, taking into consideration its condition and age, as well as the knots used in it and the purpose to which it is being put; *see also* breaking strength.

Sailmaker's whipping: not as secure as needle and palm whipping (*see* page 120), but an acceptable alternative when a needle is not available.

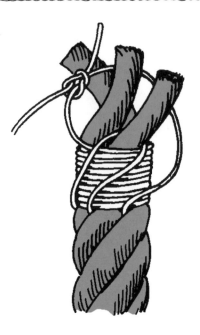

figure 111

Make a bight with the whipping twine around a single strand of rope, pulling it down to the bottom of where the whipping will begin. Then take both ends out between the other two strands, retaining a bight.

Lay all three strands of the rope together, twisting them between your thumb and forefinger if necessary to get them to lie better together. They can be held while the turns are taken with the whipping twine, working back towards the end of the rope. Now, holding the whipping tightly, take the original bight formed in the twine at the foot of the whipping, and slip it over the end of the strand it was formed around. Then haul this tight by pulling on the end projecting from the lay beneath the whipping. Weave this end to the top of the whipping and tie it with the other end of the twine (*figure 111*), pulling tight the twine to complete the whipping.

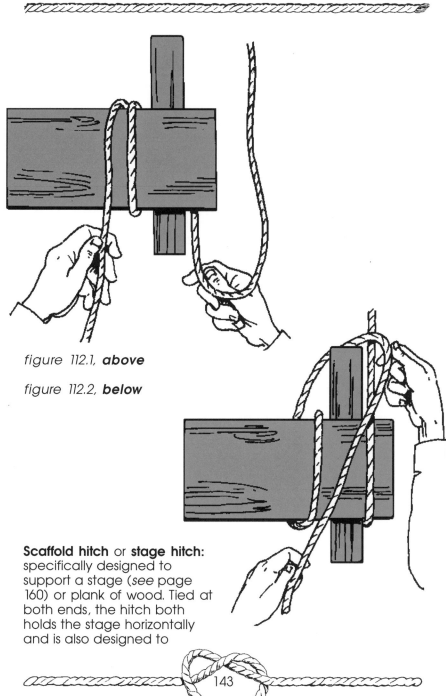

*figure 112.1, **above***

*figure 112.2, **below***

Scaffold hitch or **stage hitch:**
specifically designed to
support a stage (*see* page
160) or plank of wood. Tied at
both ends, the hitch both
holds the stage horizontally
and is also designed to

figure 112.3

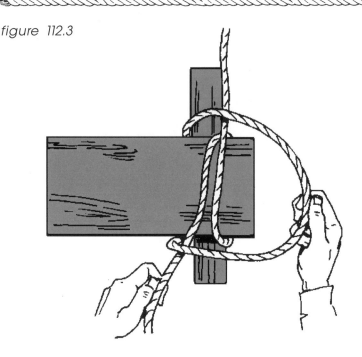

prevent it from slipping. The knot can be formed with or without horns (*see* page 96). Our illustrations show both the stage and a horn.

Take a round turn on the inside of the horn, and a second on the outside, with the rope crossing on the underside of the horn (*figure 112.1*). Then lift the first turn over the second turn and up over the top of the horn (*figure 112.2*). Next lift the original second turn over the first and third turns, and take the bight and placed it downwards over the end of the stage (*figure 112.3*). Sufficient length should be retained in the working end to make it fast with a bowline to the standing part.

Security: the knot's ability to resist slipping, distorting or capsizing when a load is applied, whether as a constant load or as a shock load.

Seizing: a lashing used to secure two ropes, or even two parts of the same rope, together; *see also* flat seizing, racking seizing and round seizing.

Sennits: braids of rope yarn, which can be divided into three basic groups – those that can be formed with any number of strands; those that can only be formed with an odd number of strands, and those that can only be formed with an even number of strands; *see also* common sennit (three-stranded), common sennit (seven-stranded), double carrick bend sennit, English sennit (seven-stranded), French sennit (four-stranded), Portuguese sennit (flat), Portuguese sennit (spiral), round sennit (four-stranded), Russian sennit (six-stranded), square sennit (eight-stranded).

Serving including *parcelling* and *worming*: a serving can be applied without either parcelling or worming; however, the latter two cannot be used without serving to finish the work.

To **worm** a rope, you lay lengths of small cordage, such as lengths of marline, in the grooves between the strands of a rope with the lay. This has the effect of infilling, to form a more even surface.

Parcelling can be applied on top of the worming, using canvas which has been waterproofed by impregnating it with tar. Bandage a strip of canvas 50 to 75mm (2 to 3in) wide around the worming, also with the lay. Take care to ensure that the windings overlap downwards, so that if they become wet, any water will run off.

Finally, apply the **serving** against the lay, by tightly binding the worming and parcelling with marline, which should be laid on with a serving mallet in order to ensure even turns with no gaps, in addition to supplying the required tightness.

Sewn whipping *see* **needle and palm whipping**.

Shamrock knot: quite a decorative knot which is of a

figure 113.1

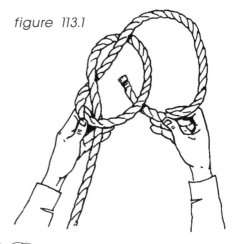

similar type in its formation to the jury mast head knot (*see* page 103), and is developed from the true lover's knot (*see* page 175).

Tie a true lover's knot (*figures 113.1–113.2*), leaving plenty of length of working end and having kept the thumb knots loose enough to be able to slip your fingers through them. Now slip your fingers through the thumb knots, taking hold of the two central interlocking pieces of rope. Pull the right central rope to the right and the left central rope to the left

through their respective thumb knots to form a bight on each side (*figure 113.3*); *see also* decorative shamrock knot.

Sheave: a grooved wheel, set within the framework of a block.

Sheep shank: a very old knot, largely now overlooked or discarded. It is used to shorten the length of a rope without cutting it, or to circumnavigate a weak or

figure 113.3, **right**

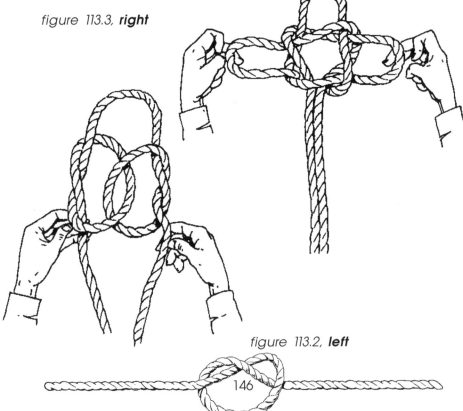

figure 113.2, **left**

figure 114.1

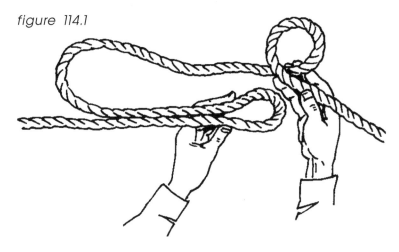

figure 114.2

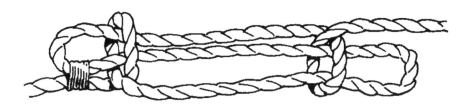

damaged portion of rope. The knot is tied in the bight of a rope, without using ends, it holds fast under tension, yet falls apart when slackened.

Form a bight in the line, make a half hitch (*see* page 91), turn it and place it over the bight (*figure 114.1*). Make another half hitch, turn that and place it over the other end. The knot is now complete (*figure 114.2*), but remember to hold it in position until the rope has taken the strain. Any damaged part of rope you are trying to bypass should be in the central section of rope, between the two loops. For additional security the bights can be seized to the standing parts.

Sheep shank (from Tom Fool's knot): another way of forming

figure 115.1, **above**

figure 115.2

a sheep shank, its only advantage being that the Tom Fool's knot holds the three parts together in an enlarged sheep shank.

First form a Tom Fool's knot (*see* page 173) (*figure 115.1*), and finish it as for the standard sheep shank by forming a half hitch at each end, turning it and passing it over the bights at the ends of the Tom Fool's knot (*figure 115.2*).

Sheep shank (pinned): although perhaps more decorative, the pinned sheep shank is no stronger than the basic version.

Start with a sheep shank formed from a Tom Fool's knot (*see* page 173), and make further bights at both ends from the standing parts. Tuck

these through the existing end bights of the knot. Pass pins or marline spikes through these last bights (*figure 116*), which are secured in position with a lashing.

figure 116, ***above***

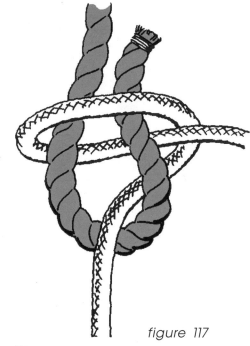

Sheet bend or **becket bend:** commonly accepted as the knot with which to join two ropes together. You should remember that when joining two ropes of different sizes the larger rope should provide the bight with the bends being made in the smaller.

Form a bight in one line, the larger if they are of differing sizes, and pass the other line through the bight before taking a turn around the neck of the bight and tucking the end under itself, so that it is trapped by its own standing part (*figure 117*).

figure 117

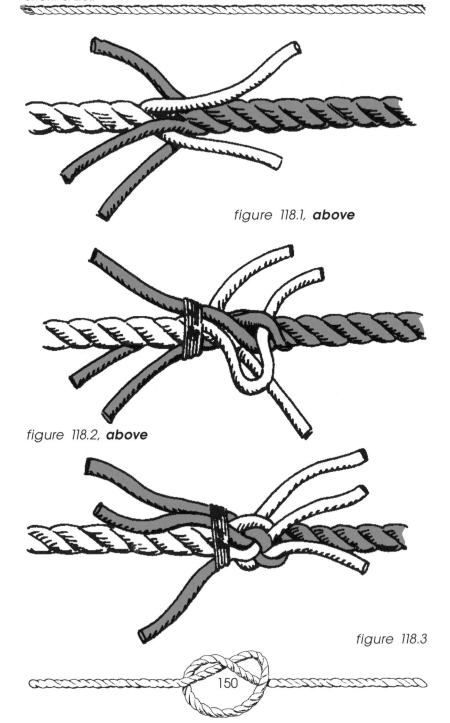

figure 118.1, **above**

figure 118.2, **above**

figure 118.3

The same knot is also called a becket bend but only when one line is attached to an eye splice in the end of another rope.

Short splice: an ideal method for joining two ropes permanently, provided that the splice does not have to be worked over a sheave because of the rope's increased diameter.

Begin by unlaying a sufficient length of strands in both rope ends and then apply a whipping of about four or five turns to the ends of the strands to stop them from fraying. Alternatively, you could apply a constrictor knot (*see* page 49).

Position the ends of the ropes opposite to each other and touching. Arrange the strands from the left-hand end to alternate with those of the right-hand end (*figure 118.1*). To keep the ropes in position temporarily, put a stop around one set of strands and the other rope (*figure 118.2*). Begin to tuck against the lay with one of the free strands, taking it over one strand and under the next. Tuck the two remaining free strands in the same manner, over one, under one (*figure 118.3*). Remove the stop and tuck the

strands into the first rope in the same manner; over one, under one, always against the lay. Working with alternate ropes, tuck the strands a couple of times more, over one, under one, against the lay. To finish the knot, trim off the ends and roll the splice under your foot to help it settle.

Shroud laid: a rope that consists of four strands, laid right-handed around a central heart.

Shrouds: the standing rigging from the mast down to the sides of a vessel.

Single tuck eye splice with wall knot finish: a decorative eye splice. It is formed initially

figure 119.1

like the basic eye splice (*see page 76*) by unlaying the rope a short way, but further than you would for the eye splice, and sealing the ends of the strands.

Take the middle unlaid strand and tuck it under one strand of the standing part, against the lay, at a point that provides you with a bight of the size you require. Next take the strand lying on the inside, and tuck it under the next strand of the standing part (*figure 119.1*) at the same point along the rope. The

third strand needs to be turned back towards itself so that it can also be tucked against the lay, in the same position as the first.

Next form a wall knot (*see page 187*) around the standing part (*figure 119.2*) by passing each strand in turn around and under its neighbour, working with the lay. The end of the final strand is passed upwards through the bight formed by the first.

figure 119.2

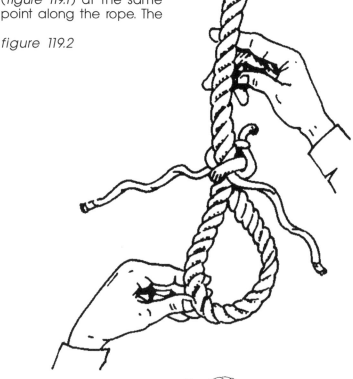

figure 120

The wall is followed around once more and finished by hauling tight all the working strands and trimming off the tails close to the knot.

'S' laid rope: rope manufactured with a left-handed lay.

Sliding figures of eight: a knot which joins two ropes together securely, even if they are of different sizes, and yet this knot is easy to undo.

Form two figures of eight (*see* page 80), one in the end of each rope, with the opposing line being contained in the lower loop of each figure of eight (*figure 120*). To finish, tighten each figure of eight

and slide them together by applying tension to each standing part.

Sling: cordage of any description that is applied around an object, usually in the form of an endless band, to hoist or haul it; *see also* strop.

Slip knot: a useful stopper knot, and a good way to start tying a parcel.

Start to form a thumb knot (*see* page 171), but pull through only a bight taken in the working end, instead of the whole working end. This bight is then secured by the thumb knot when tightened.

figure 121

Slipped reef knot: the slip contained within the reef knot enables the knot to be undone in a hurry by simply pulling on the slipped end.

Form it in the same way as a reef knot (*see* page 130), left over right, right over left, but without pulling through one end, leaving it as a bight which is then secured (*figure 121*) like a reef bow used for tying shoe laces (*see* page 130).

Soft lay or **loose lay:** a rope is said to be soft laid when it has been loosely twisted.

figure 122.1

Spanish bowline: made on the bight, it is put to good use where conditions call for both of the standing parts to be under load.

Begin by finding the centre of the rope, and lay it out as three bights (*figure 122.1*) with the much larger central bight formed with the left part over the right, while the two smaller outer bights are turned inwards. Take the top bight and fold it down to lie across the other two bights and the two standing parts (*figure 122.2*). Now spread the outer edges of the larger bight outwards to encompass the two smaller bights, up through which you bring these outer edges of the larger bight (*figure 122.3*). Pull them well through before working the whole knot tight (*figure 122.4*) by pulling on both these and on both ends at the same

figure 122.2

figure 122.3

figure 122.4

155

time. The two outer loops, which can be pulled away from the standing parts in the opposite direction, will then support separate loads.

Spar hitch: possibly better than either a clove hitch (*see* page 40) because it is more secure, or a constrictor knot (*see* page 49), because it is easier to undo.

To form a spar hitch, take a turn around the post, passing the end over the standing part, and then once more around the post in the same direction. The end is then crossed back over the standing part and tucked under the rope at the point

where it first crosses the post (*figure 123*).

Splice: used to join together two ropes, whether they are ends of different ropes or to overcome a damaged section within a single rope. In addition, they can encompass an eye before being joined back to themselves; *see also* Admiralty eye splice, back splice, bargee's eye splice, bulldog splice, chain splice, cut splice, eye splice, eye splice (in the middle of a rope), Liverpool eye splice, long splice, marlow eye splice, short splice, single tuck eye splice.

figure 123

figure 124.1

Spunyarn *see* **marline**.

Square knot: made in two ropes, this is a symmetrical decorative knot with four standing parts, all of which go in different directions.

Form a bight in each of the ropes and pass one through the other at right angles. Then take the farther end of the rope forming the outer bight and pass it up through the end of the inner bight (*figure 124.1*). Now take the lower working end of the rope forming the end of the inner bight around the standing part of the outer bight and on through the second bight formed in the other rope (*figure 124.2*). At this point the knot should look like interlocking letter Ss, and now you can work tight the knot

figure 124.2

by hauling carefully on all ends.

NB: *in America the square knot is not as described here but is as the reef knot (see page 130).*

Square lashing: used to hold two spars or posts together when they are crossed at right angles.

Begin by forming a clove hitch (*see* page 40) around the horizontal post with one end of the rope, leaving a long end of the rope which will be used to form the lashing. Begin this by taking the rope back around the top of the second, vertical, spar, and then forward down across the horizontal spar and back behind the lower part of the vertical spar from where it emerges beside the front of the clove hitch (*figure 125*). This completes a full round of lashing which you should

figure 125

repeat several times, hauling tight each round until the posts are securely held together. Finish off with a half hitch.

Square plait: easier and quicker to make than a

square sennit, this has the added advantage of being formed on a single strand.

Begin by forming a Tom Fool's knot (*see* page 173) (*figure 126.1*)., after which you should make a bight in the standing part and pull it through the loop on the right-hand side, securing it there by pulling back on the strand of the left-hand loop (*figure 126.2*).

Repeat the process by taking a bight through the left-hand loop, which you haul tight by one strand of the right-hand loop. You continue working alternately until the required length is reached (*figure 126.3*).

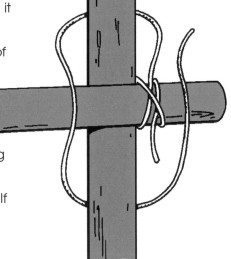

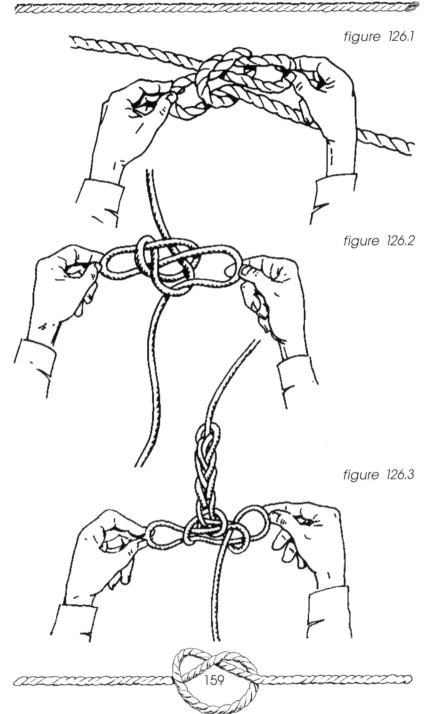

figure 126.1

figure 126.2

figure 126.3

To finish pass the end, not a bight, through the penultimate loop and back through the last loop. The plait will not then unravel.

Square sennit (eight-stranded): an unusual sennit in that it must be made not only with an even number of strands, but also with multiples of four strands. Eight strands, as illustrated, are the minimum workable.

Secure the strands at the top, leaving yourself sufficient space with which to work. The sennit can be hauled tight later. Now separate the strands into two equal groups; these are groups of four in our illustrated version.

Begin by taking the outside right strand under its right-hand side fellows and on to come up through the centre of the left-hand set of four, taking it around these two strands to lie on the inside of the right-hand side set of strands; it will now be the fourth strand in from the right. Now take the outside left strand and repeat the movement; under its fellows, on under two of the right-hand side strands, up and around to be laid back in the left centre position, that is, four strands in from the left.

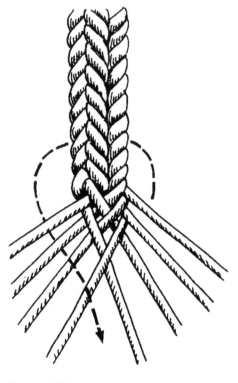

figure 127

Continue now to form the sennit working with alternate outside strands until you reach the required length (*figure 127*), when you should hitch together the strands at the top and haul tight the sennit.

Stage: a plank of timber which is suspended as a working platform; *see also* horn and scaffold hitch.

Stage hitch *see* **scaffold hitch**.

Standing end: the other end of the rope to the working end.

Standing part: the remaining part of a rope, other than the

figure 128

figure 129.1

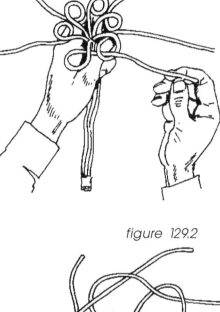

STANDING PART

figure 129.2

ends, or bight or that piece of rope that is being employed in the tying of a knot. It is usually that part that is under load (*figure 128*).

Staple: graded fibres or finely chopped filaments used in rope making, which produce a rope with a fuzzy surface as a result of all the ends.

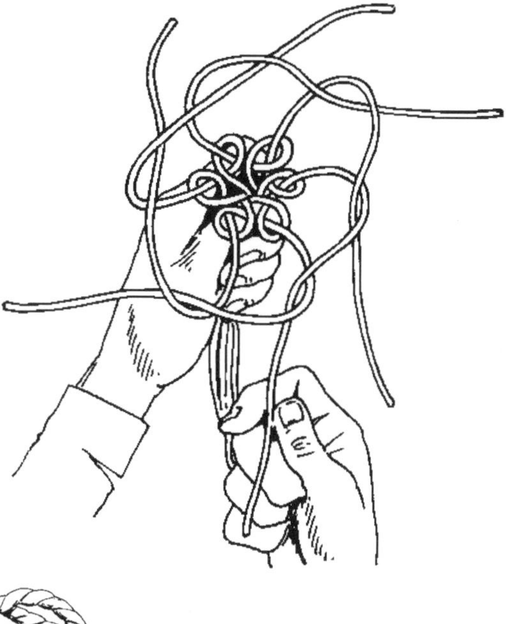

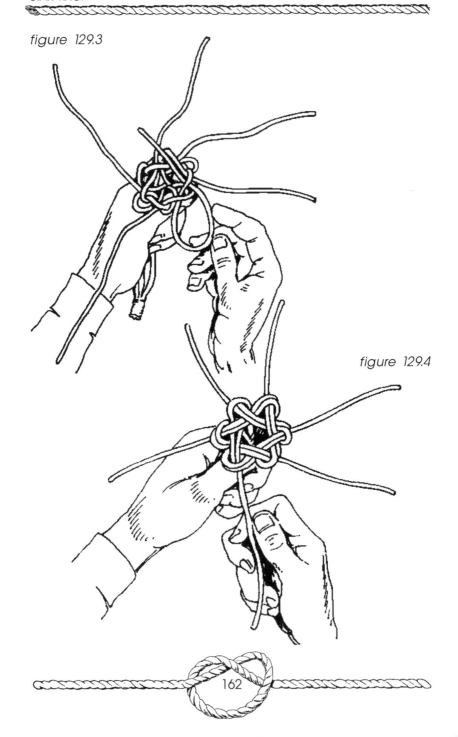

figure 129.3

figure 129.4

Star knot (six-stranded): a useful decorative knot which needs patience to begin with, but the end result is well worth the effort.

Holding all six strands in your left hand, loop each one backwards, then pass each end up through the next anticlockwise loop (*figure 129.1*); *see also* crown knot page 57. Then crown all strands backwards clockwise (*figure 129.2*). Now take each strand, and working anticlockwise again, bring it back around and up under itself (*figure 129.3*), the effect of which is to form a second layer of six loops immediately above the first set. Work the knot close.

You will notice that each strand is now lying alongside a previous bight, and lies over a pair of loops. Tuck each strand down through the

figure 130.1

same loop as its adjacent bight (*figure 129.4*). You must now turn the knot upside down, where the emerging strands will again lie adjacent to a previous bight. Tuck each strand down through the same loop as its adjacent bight again, and out through the centre of the knot, so that they all emerge at the top of the knot.

Stitch and whip eye: an alternative to splicing, used to make an eye in plaited rope. You will need a thimble and about 3m (10ft) of thick whipping twine.

Begin by forming a bight in the rope for the eye, and insert the thimble, leaving yourself about 75mm (3in) of tail. Using a sail needle

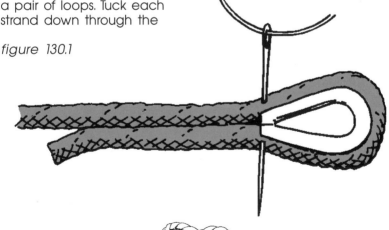

figure 130.2

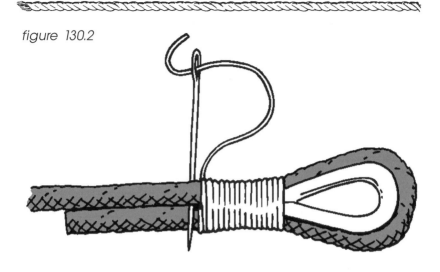

threaded with the whipping twine, take a stitch with the needle as close to the throat of the thimble as you can (*figure 130.1*), taking all of the twine through with the exception of about 50mm (2in).

Sew up to the end of the tail with diagonal stitches about every 15mm (0.5in), and then sew back to the throat of the thimble again, at which point the 50mm (2in) end of the twine that was left behind when the first stitch was made can now be cut short, and the two parts of the rope should be hammered together to ensure that the rope is tightly drawn about the thimble.

Start the whipping as close to the thimble as possible, working away from the eye. When half way along, take a stitch through the standing part of the rope (*figure 130.2*) and then continue the whipping, ensuring that it is tightly wound and that all turns are taken snugly together. At the end make five or six stitches through the standing part of the rope at an angle of 45 degrees, sewing away from the eye, to secure the twine. The surplus twine can now be cut off and the eye is complete.

Stopper knot: as the name suggests, this is a knot that must not slip through a block, or indeed out of your hand.

figure 131.2, **below**

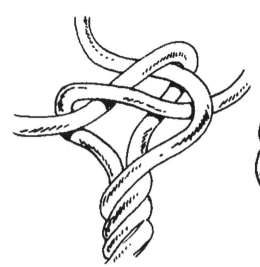

figure 131.1

It is made by first forming a crown knot (*see* page 57) (*figure 131.1*), which is followed by a wall knot (*see* page 187); because the strands from the crown hang down, the wall is made under the crown.

Follow around the crown knot first then follow around the wall, and finish by taking the strands out at the sides or through the centre of the knot, where they can be trimmed off (*figure 131.2*).

A much simpler stopper knot can be formed by starting as for a figure of eight (*see* page 80), but making an extra half twist before tucking the end.

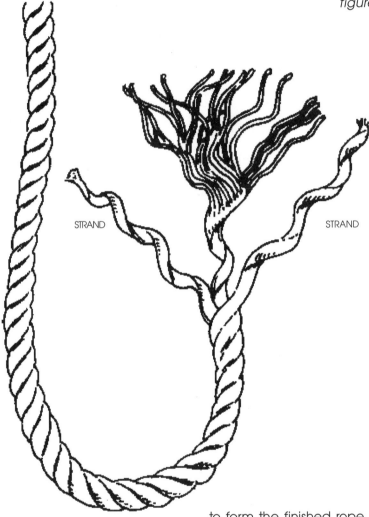

figure 132

STRAND

STRAND

Strands: yarns are twisted together in the opposite direction to the lay of the yarn itself, to form strands. The appropriate number of strands are twisted together to form the finished rope (*figure 132*); *see also* rope, yarns, and fibres.

Strangle knot: essentially a transom knot (*see* page 175) which has been allocated a

separate name because it is
tied around a single post.

Form a round turn around the
post but initially taking the
end in a diagonal direction,
right to left, across the post. It
will then be trapped when the
line is brought back across the
front of the post, also in a
diagonal direction but this
time from left to right. The
working end will then hang
down behind the post and
between the standing part
and the bottom of the first
turn. Now bring the end up
across the standing part and
tuck it under both turns at the
top, hauling it tight to secure.

String: usually refers to thin
cordage for domestic use
and includes thick thread and
twine.

Strop: a rope or wire strap
that is seized around a pulley
block to suspend it; *see also*
sling.

Surgeon's knot: originally used
by surgeons to tie off blood
vessels; this knot now has a
much wider use because of its
ability to hold much better
than the reef knot (*see* page
130) in slippery synthetic fibres.

The knot looks rather like an
elongated reef knot. Form it
by first making a thumb knot
in one end and then giving
one of the ends an extra turn
around the other. Then make
a second thumb knot, but this
time in the opposite direction,
and again with an extra turn.
The finished knot is illustrated
in *figure 133*.

Synthetic rope: rope made
from man made fibres or
staples. They are damp proof
and have immense strength.
They also possess a great
resistance to weathering and
attack by chemicals; *see also*
Kevlar, monofilament,

figure 133

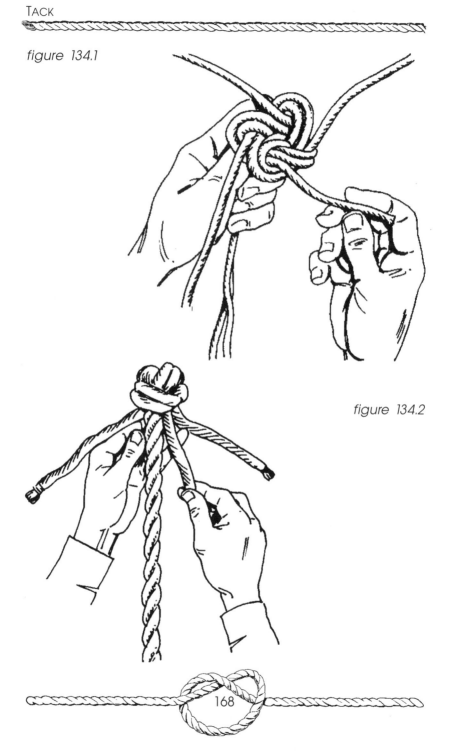

figure 134.1

figure 134.2

168

polyamide (nylon), polyester, polyethylene, and polypropylene.

T

Tack: the lower, forward corner of a fore and aft sail.

Tack knot: a decorative knot which looks rather similar to the manrope and stopper knots (*see* pages 113 and 164 respectively). It is often confused with them and its formation is even begun in the same manner.

Unlay the strands for a few turns and then apply a double wall (*see* page 72) by passing each strand around under its neighbour, working anticlockwise, and pass the last strand up through the bight of the first. Take the emerging strands and follow around until all again emerge separately from the top and are pointing upwards (*figure 134.1*).

Now add a double crown (*see* page 69) by passing each strand around over its neighbour working anticlockwise, with the last strand being passed down through the bight of the first. All strands will now emerge at the bottom pointing

downwards. Now pull each one back to make an anticlockwise turn around the strand it has passed over, thus returning it to its original position, with the last passing through the double bight of the first. Then tuck the ends down through the knot (*figure 134.2*), taper them and finally serve (*see* page 145) to finish.

Tag end *see* **bare end, end**.

Tail or **tail end:** the extreme ends of a rope or any of its individual strands; *see also* bitter end, end and standing end.

Tail end *see* **tail**.

Terylene *see* **polyester**.

Thief knot *see* **draw hitch**.

Thimble: a metal or plastic loop, U-shaped in cross-

figure 135

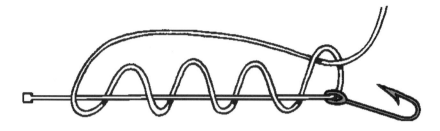

figure 136

section to hold the rope in position, used to help in forming an eye (*figure 135*).

Thread: a yarn or fine line used for sewing.

Three and a half turn clinch knot or **half blood knot:** useful for attaching a hook to a thicker line and where the five turns of the improved half blood knot (*see* page 19) will not tighten snugly.

Pass the end through the eye

of the hook and take three and a half turns around its standing part, before bringing the end back through the first turn next to the eye of the hook (*figure 136*). To tighten the knot, first dampen the knot and hold the hook by means of a pair of pliers in your right hand. If you are using heavy monofilament line, use a rag around your hand to grip the standing part of the line, both to increase the purchase on the line and to protect your hand. Pull

figure 137

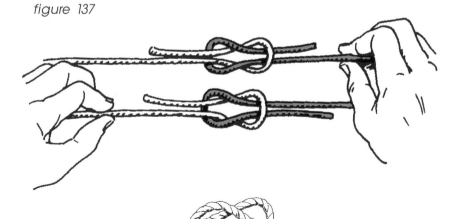

170

steadily on the standing part, and finish by trimming the end.

'Threef' knot: a reef knot to all intents and purposes, except that it has been mis-tied. With the reef knot (*see* page 130) both ends emerge on the top side of the knot; however, here one finishes at the top and the other finishes at the bottom.

Form a bight in the left-hand rope, with the working end at the top. Pass the end of the other rope upwards through this bight and take a turn around both parts of the first (left-hand side) rope. Now take the end back down through the bight on the bottom side of its standing part (*figure 137, bottom*).

This knot is used as a telltale knot; should the original threef be untied by a thief, the chances are that he or she would tie it up again correctly as a reef knot, thereby disclosing the fact that the knot and the item that it held closed had been disturbed.

Thumb knot: or **overhand knot:** the simplest of stopper knots, and not particularly useful on its own except for tying parcels.

Form a bight by crossing the end over the standing part of the rope. Draw the end upwards through this bight. Alternatively, start with an overhand loop and bring the end up through it to complete the knot; with an underhand loop you push the end down through the loop (*figure 138*).

figure 138

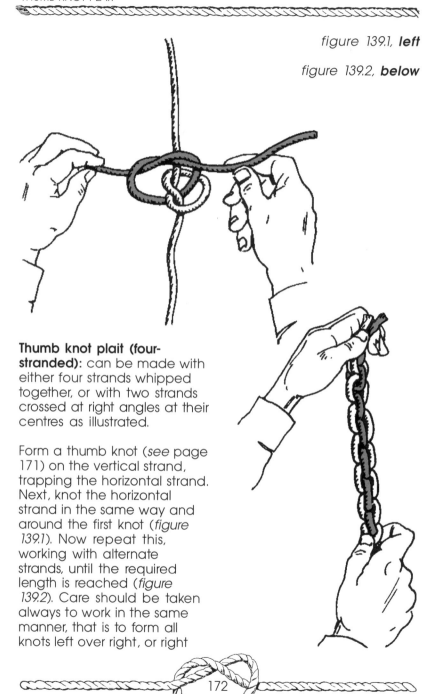

Thumb knot plait (four-stranded): can be made with either four strands whipped together, or with two strands crossed at right angles at their centres as illustrated.

Form a thumb knot (*see* page 171) on the vertical strand, trapping the horizontal strand. Next, knot the horizontal strand in the same way and around the first knot (*figure 139.1*). Now repeat this, working with alternate strands, until the required length is reached (*figure 139.2*). Care should be taken always to work in the same manner, that is to form all knots left over right, or right over left, or alternately. Do not tie them randomly.

The plait can also be made on eight strands, which should be laid out as crossing pairs of strands, about 25mm (1in) apart with the thumb knots tied around both the crossing strands in pairs, to make a doubled version of the four-stranded plait.

Tight lay *see* **hard lay**.

Timber hitch: a simple temporary hitch used for dragging planks; when using it, it is important that the noose holds tight.

Pass the end of the rope around the timber and then around its own standing part. Then twist the end back down this bight (*figure 140*); *see also* dog, killick hitch.

Tom Fool's knot or **fool's knot:** the knot itself is a trick knot, but it is important because it forms the basis of other more practical knots such as the chair harness, pinned sheep shank and sheep shank from

figure 140

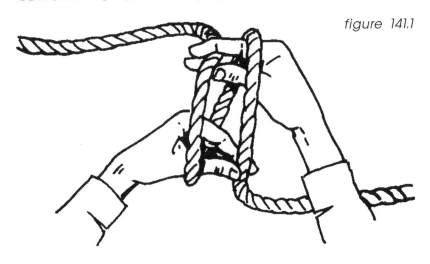

figure 141.1

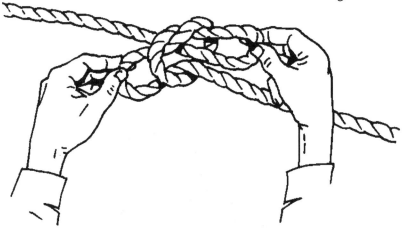

figure 141.2

a Tom fool's knot (*see* pages 37, 148 and 147 respectively).

The knot is made in the centre of a rope by taking a turn around your left hand, from the top, and around your

right hand. With your left hand positioned below your right hand, hold the rope in your right fingers above your left hand and in your left fingers below your right hand (*figure 141.1*), and pull your hands apart taking the turns with them (*figure 141.2*). This forms the finished knot, around the centre of two bights.

Topping lift: the running rigging from the mast to the outer end of a beam, usually set in pairs, one on each side of the sail. These relieve the sail from the weight of the beam.

Transom knot: an excellent way of fixing together two crossed pieces of wood or garden canes.

Lay the standing part along the length of one of the pieces of wood and hold it

there with your thumb. Now take the end up along the piece of wood, crossing over the cross piece of wood. Continue by taking a turn around the back of the first piece, back down diagonally across the standing part, to take another turn around the back of the first piece of wood, but this time below the cross piece. Bring the end forward under the turn just completed, and under the first turn, to lie along the first piece of wood.

True lover's knot: a decorative knot of little practical value,

figure 142.1

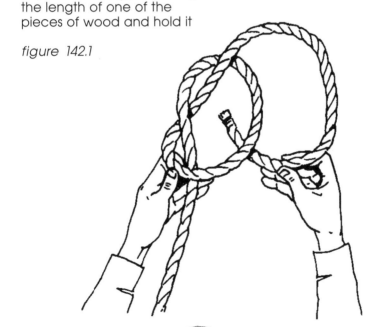

sometimes tied in small cord to form a lanyard for wearing around the neck, which could support a stop watch or a locket. The knot also forms the basis for the shamrock knot, and is related to the jury mast head knot; it is comprised of two interlocking thumb knots.

To form this knot, first make one thumb knot and then pass the working end up through the bight of the knot (*figure 142.1*) before forming a second thumb knot in the second bight (*figure 142.2*).

figure 142.2

Tucked half blood knot *see* **improved clinch knot**.

Tucking: the action of passing the working end of a strand over a strand of the standing part of a rope. When you take it under the next strand in the opposite direction to the lay of the rope this is called tucking against the lay. To tuck with the lay, the working end is passed around any strand of the standing part in the same direction as the lay.

Turk's head: a purely decorative piece of ropework, it is probably the

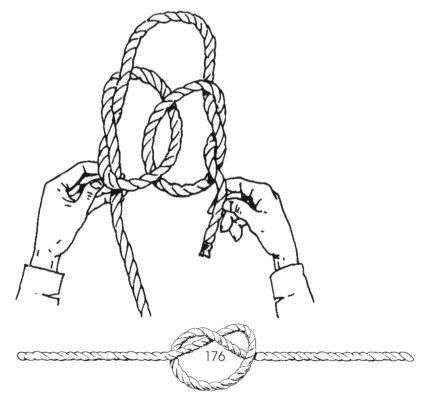

best known of all fancy knots, being quite easy to form.

We have illustrated the formation on the hand for flexibility and clarity, but in practice the Turk's head

would be applied directly around the object.

Take a round turn around the object as if proceeding to make a clove hitch (*see* page 40), but instead of tucking the

figure 143.1

figure 143.2

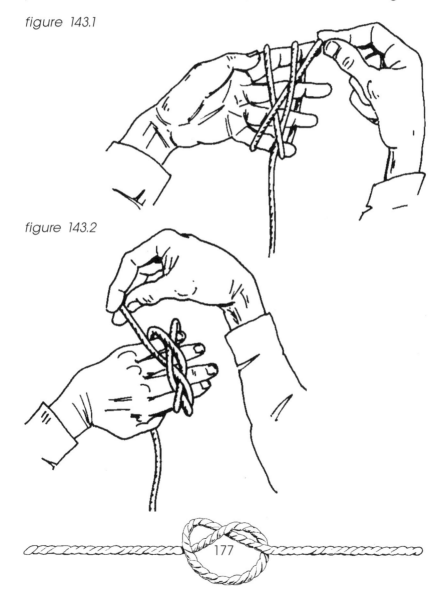

standing end to lie parallel, pass it across the standing part and tuck it under the first upward part of the first turn (*figure 143.1*).

At this point the turns behind the hand (the object) are lying parallel to each other. Now cross these left over right and take the working end up and to tuck it between them from right to left (*figure 143.2*), and then down between the gap between the two parts lying over the top of the little finger in *figure 143.2*, where it emerges at the bottom of the front of the hand, lying alongside the standing part.

Next follow around, passing the working end under and over around the knot for a

second time, following exactly the course of the first turns. The end will then be already pointing in the correct direction for a second follow around (*figure 143.3*). After this, the ends are cut short and they can be hidden under the turns at the point of origin.

Turk's head (with ten extra turns): a more elaborate version of the basic Turk's head (*see* page 176). It is made possible by increasing the parts and turns, the number of times the knot is followed around being a matter of choice (*figure 144*).

figure 143.3

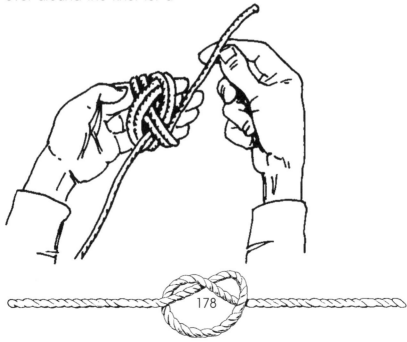

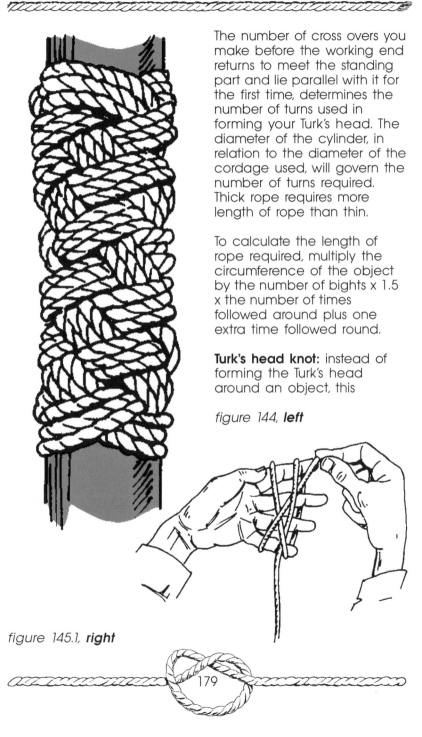

The number of cross overs you make before the working end returns to meet the standing part and lie parallel with it for the first time, determines the number of turns used in forming your Turk's head. The diameter of the cylinder, in relation to the diameter of the cordage used, will govern the number of turns required. Thick rope requires more length of rope than thin.

To calculate the length of rope required, multiply the circumference of the object by the number of bights x 1.5 x the number of times followed around plus one extra time followed round.

Turk's head knot: instead of forming the Turk's head around an object, this

*figure 144, **left***

*figure 145.1, **right***

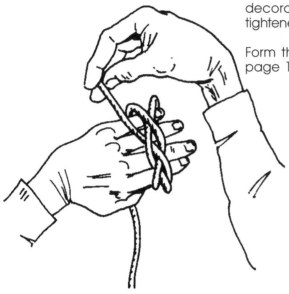

decorative knot has been tightened to form a ball.

Form the Turk's head (*see* page 176) by taking a round

figure 145.2, **above**

figure 145.3, **below**

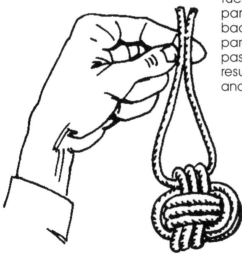

turn, crossing the standing part before taking a second turn, and passing that over the first crossing part but tucking it under the standing part (*figure 145.1*). At the back of the hand cross the parallel turns left over right, pass the end through the resultant space (*figure 145.2*), and down through the next gap between the parts to lay next to the standing part. Follow around twice more before working the whole into a tight ball (*figure 145.3*).

Turle knot: designed to create a straight pull on any hook where the fly has a turned down eye.

To form it, pass the end through the hook's eye and make a bight around which you tie a thumb knot (*see* page 171). Now bring the

Turn: when the rope being worked is passed around another piece of rope or a post in a single bight, coming back on itself in a full 360 degrees so that the ropes cross. The act of doing this is called taking a turn; *see also* forming a knot.

Twenty times around knot *see* **Bimini twist**.

Twist plait: a useful plait, because it is made in a single rope.

figure 146

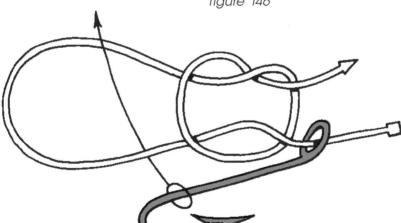

hook up through the bight (*figure 146*), drawing the knot snug on the upper side of the neck of the hook. Be careful to avoid catching the hackles of the fly.

Begin by making a large bight; the size of the bight dictates the length of the plait. Take a turn around the standing part, and pass the end down through the bight.

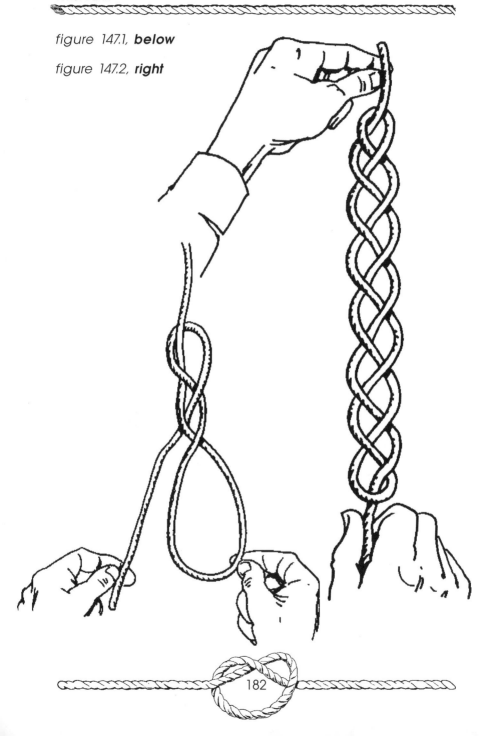

figure 147.1, **below**

figure 147.2, **right**

Now twist the bight anticlockwise (*figure 147.1*), and tuck the end through the (now smaller) bight. Continue twisting and tucking until you run out of bight (*figure 147.2*).

Two half hitches *see* **round turn and two half hitches**.

U

Underhand loop *see* **overhand loop**.

Unlay: the action of untwisting the individual strands of a rope, *see* splices.

figure 148.1, **below**

figure 148.2, **right**

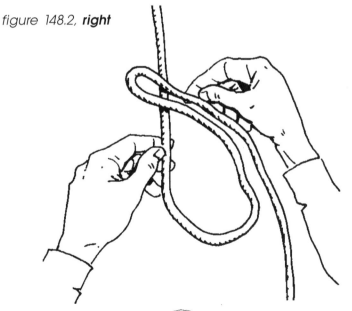

W

Wagoner's hitch or **lorry driver's hitch:** a traditional method used by lorry drivers to lash down loads, it combines a knot with a purchase which allows the standing part to be bowsed down (*see* page 23) really tightly.

Form a small bight in the working end and pass this

figure 148.3, **below**

figure 148.4, **right**

over the standing part (*figure 148.1*). Now take a round turn around the bight with the standing part (*figure 148.2*), which provides a larger second bight. Twist this bight anticlockwise (*figure 148.3*). Form another bight in the working end, passing this through the remaining loop of the twisted bight. This last bight in the end of the rope can be used to drop over a hook (in our illustration *figure 148.4*, a finger) to provide purchase when the end is secured.

figure 149.1

Wall and crown knot: exactly as it says, a combination of a wall knot (*see* page 187) followed by a crown knot (*see* page 57).

Form the wall first by passing each strand around and under its neighbour, working anticlockwise, passing the last strand upwards through the bight of the first strand (*figure 149. 1*). All strands will emerge separately from the top, where you make a crown knot. Do this by passing each strand around over its neighbour, again working anticlockwise, passing the last strand down through the

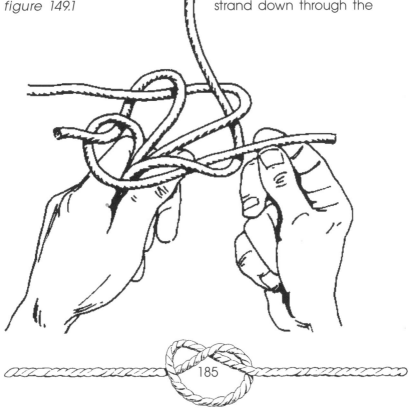

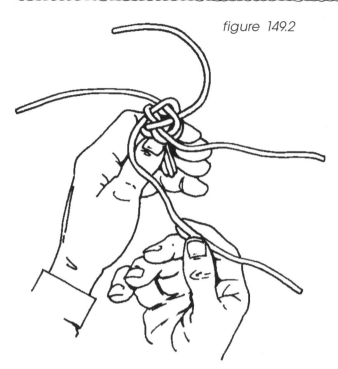

figure 149.2

bight of the first (*figure 149.2*), and cut short all of the ends to finish the knot.

Wall and crown plait: a continuation from the wall and crown knot (*see* page 184), whereby instead of cutting the ends short at the completion of the knot, you continue to form alternate wall and crown knots to make a plait (*figure 150*). If this is being made around a cylindrical object, the ends of the strands can be made secure by seizing them to the object.

NB the wall and crown plait cannot be made with more than four strands.

Walling: we have illustrated the wall knot as formed at the end of a length of three-stranded rope. However, you can wall any number of strands and to demonstrate this, *figure 149.1* of the **wall and crown knot** shows the wall formed from four strands. The same method is used for any number of strands, with each strand being passed around under its neighbour working anticlockwise, with

the last strand passed up through the bight of the first; *see also* continuous walling.

Wall knot: often referred to as 'a wall', this knot is quite simply a crown knot (*see* page 57) made upside down.

You can make it by passing each strand around and under its neighbour, working anticlockwise, with the last strand being passed upwards through the bight of the first strand (*figure 151.1*). If you are working in the end of a rope, unlay the rope to the required length, and work the wall with the lay. Unlike the crown knot,

figure 151.1

figure 150

the strands of the wall will all emerge from the top (*figure 151.2*). Like the crown though, this is seldom used on its own;

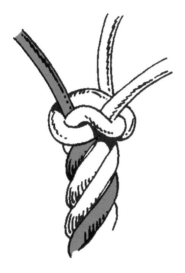

figure 151.2

see manrope, double wall knot and Matthew Walker knot.

Wall plait: a continuation from the wall knot (*see* page 187), it is formed without a central heart by forming one wall knot after another. As with the wall and crown plait, no more than four strands can be used to form the plait (*figure 152*).

Weaver's knot: used to join a fresh piece of wool onto a broken end.

figure 152

Cross the lines at right angles, forming a bight in the top line back over the bottom line.

figure 153

Take a turn around this, bringing the working end of the top line up through the bight and lying it parallel to its standing part. Now bring the end of the bottom line over the top line and down between the other end and the neck of the bight (*figure 153*). Haul tight on both standing parts to lock the knot.

West country whipping: a particularly good whipping when applied with synthetic fibre whipping twine.

Form a thumb knot (*see* page 171) around the end of the rope, with the middle of the twine (*figure 154.1*). Take the twine to the back of the rope and tie a second thumb knot

figure 154.1

opposite the first. Return the twine to the front and tie a third knot immediately above the first, followed by a fourth at the back immediately

figure 154.2

above the second, a fifth at the front, and so on until you reach the end of the rope (*figure 154.2*). The ends of the twine are finished off with either a reef knot (*see* page 130) or a surgeon's knot (*see* page 167).

Whipping: a series of turns made with sail twine or similar thread, which are bound tightly to form a lashing at the end of a rope or an individual strand, to prevent fraying or unlaying; *see also* coach whipping, common whipping, French whipping, needle and palm whipping, sailmaker's whipping, west country whipping

Wire eye splice *see* **Liverpool eye splice**.

Working end *see* **end**.

Worming *see* **serving**.

Wrap *see* **turns**.

Y

Yarn: fibres or filaments are twisted together to form the yarn. Yarns are twisted together in the opposite direction to form strands, in the second stage of rope making (*figure 155*).

Z

Zeppelin bend *see* **hunter's bend**.

'Z' laid rope: rope manufactured with a right-handed lay.

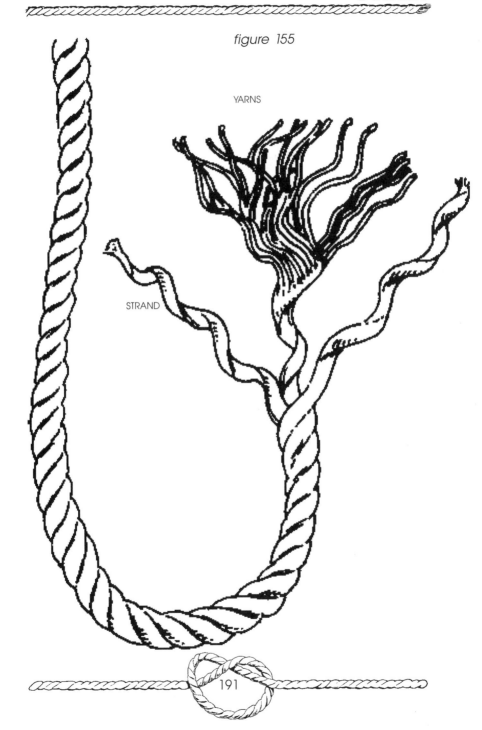

figure 155

YARNS

STRAND